U.S. COUNTERTERRORISM IN SUB-SAHARAN AFRICA: UNDERSTANDING COSTS, CULTURES, AND CONFLICTS

Donovan C. Chau

September 2008

*****

The views expressed in this report are those of the author and do not necessarily reflect the official policy or position of the Department of the Army, the Department of Defense, or the U.S. Government. This report is cleared for public release; distribution is unlimited.

*****

Comments pertaining to this report are invited and should be forwarded to: Director, Strategic Studies Institute, U.S. Army War College, 122 Forbes Ave, Carlisle, PA 17013-5244.

*****

FOREWORD

While sub-Saharan Africa (SSA) has never been the centerpiece of U.S. foreign or defense policy, the current struggle of the United States and its allies against terrorist groups and individuals motivated by Islamic extremism has elevated the region to a front in the global conflict.

In this Letort Paper, Dr. Donovan C. Chau examines U.S. counterterrorism policy in SSA. He begins by analyzing the policy debate in Washington, DC, especially the fundamental divergence of approaches between development and defense. From there, the paper shifts to a discussion of the attitudes and views of terrorism and counterterrorism in SSA. Vast and diverse, SSA is divided subregionally into East, West, and Southern Africa so as to highlight the different geographies, histories, threats, and perceptions.

Given the debate in Washington and the perspectives from SSA, Dr. Chau answers the central question concerning the most effective long-term approach to counterterrorism in SSA. He suggests a grand strategic approach to attain "three standards" that comprise seizing and holding the moral high ground, winning the struggle for perceived legitimacy, and pursuing restrained counterterrorism responses. None of the standards are attainable, however, without a future generation of analysts, officers, and policymakers with deep knowledge and understanding of SSA.

DOUGLAS C. LOVELACE, JR.
Director
Strategic Studies Institute

iii

BIOGRAPHICAL SKETCH OF THE AUTHOR

DONOVAN C. CHAU is an Assistant Professor of Political Science and a faculty member in the National Security Studies program (M.A.) at California State University, San Bernardino. His areas of teaching and research include international politics, strategic studies, terrorism, Africa, and East Asia. He has been an Adjunct Faculty member in the Department of Defense and Strategic Studies, Missouri State University. In addition, Dr. Chau was a subject matter expert in the Counter-Terrorism and Preparedness Solutions Division of AMTI, an operation of SAIC. He was hired as the area specialist responsible for supervising and conducting research on terrorist threats in and emanating from the continent of Africa for the Department of Homeland Security's Universal Adversary program and the National Planning Scenarios. Prior to joining AMTI, Dr. Chau was a Professional Staff Member on the Committee on Homeland Security, U.S. House of Representatives. He conducted policy oversight as well as research and analysis on border and transportation security issues. Dr. Chau earned a Ph.D. in Politics and International Relations from the University of Reading (United Kingdom), an M.S. in Defense and Strategic Studies from Missouri State University, and a B.A. in Literature/Government from Claremont McKenna College.

SUMMARY

What is the most effective long-term approach to U.S. counterterrorism in sub-Saharan Africa (SSA)? The purpose of this paper is to lay the framework for answering this central question. The current struggle of the United States and its allies against terrorist groups and individuals motivated by Islamic extremism consumes U.S. military, intelligence, and law enforcement agencies. Never a centerpiece of U.S. foreign and defense policy, SSA is now a front in the conflict to counter global Islamic extremism. As in the past, however, SSA remains largely misunderstood and misperceived in the United States. Yet, the U.S. Government (USG) is now embarked on reform of U.S. policy toward the African continent with uncertain consequences.

Following an introduction (Section I), this Letort Paper next analyzes the policy debate in Washington, DC. The focus is on two fundamentally divergent theoretical approaches to U.S. counterterrorism policy in SSA—development and defense. The former prescribes civilian countermeasures; the latter, military. Examples of the development approach to counterterrorism in SSA range from humanitarian aid to financial and legal assistance to law enforcement training; the approach does not involve the use of the military. In contrast, the defense approach involves any and all uses of the military; this includes the use of the military for nonmilitary purposes such as humanitarian assistance and intervention. Section II, "The Debate in Washington," considers the benefits and costs of the defense approach; the benefits and costs of the development approach; and the metrics for success and failure. What becomes clear is that both metrics-oriented U.S. counterterrorism approaches do not account fully for the patterns and complexities throughout SSA. Furthermore, the extent to which U.S. policy has countered terrorism in the region remains unclear.

Only through recognition and understanding of the diverse perspectives across SSA may sound counterterrorism policy be formulated. From the debate in Washington, therefore, the paper moves across the Atlantic Ocean to discuss the attitudes and views of terrorism and counterterrorism in SSA. Due to geographic size and scope, SSA is divided into East, West, and Southern Africa subregions so as to highlight the different geographies, histories, threats, and perceptions. Section III, "The Perspectives from SSA," examines African views of terrorism and counterterrorism; the current state of civil-military and civil-law enforcement relations; and, ultimately, what counterterrorism is in SSA, and what counterterrorism means to Africans themselves. Discussion of perspectives from the three subregions suggests the paramount importance of understanding local identities and cultures, as well as the variegated influence of history on views of terrorism and counterterrorism.

Based on the research and findings, the paper concludes with Section IV which provides a summary and recommendations for a new grand strategic approach to U.S. counterterrorism in the region, which should focus on attaining three standards:

1. **Seizing and holding the moral high ground.** Seizing the moral high ground does not mean conducting actions better than the enemy. Rather, it means understanding what is moral in SSA and striving to achieve that level of morality in all policy considerations and actions.

2. **Winning the struggle for perceived legitimacy.**
Much like morality, legitimacy varies from one group
or individual to another. What is crucial here for U.S.
counterterrorism policy is to understand perceptions
from subregion to subregion, country to country, and
small folk community to small folk community.

3. **Pursuing restrained counterterrorism responses.**
After a terrorist attack, how the USG and the Department of Defense (DoD), in particular, respond is critical.
The main point of restrained counterterrorism responses is the need for unity of effort.

Beyond the three standards, the paper recommends
that the USG think long-term continually, build meaningful relationships in SSA, move counterterrorism
beyond DoD-centric operations, and, most importantly,
educate future analysts, officers, and policymakers
about the African continent. What should be borne
in mind throughout, and is often lost in the U.S.
policymaking process, is that foreign governments
and peoples do not often view the world according to
Western liberal values, attitudes, and beliefs. This is as
true in counterterrorism as it is in any other strategic
issue.

U.S. COUNTERTERRORISM IN SUB-SAHARAN AFRICA: UNDERSTANDING COSTS, CULTURES, AND CONFLICTS

There seems to be a number of Christopher Columbuses setting out from the United States to discover Africa for the first time. I've got news for them. It's been there for a long time.

U.K. Prime Minister
James Callaghan
May 31, 1978[1]

I. INTRODUCTION

The conflict of the United States and its allies against terrorist groups and individuals motivated by Islamic extremism consumes U.S. military, intelligence, and law enforcement agencies. Whether named the Global War on Terror (or Terrorism) (GWOT), the Long War, or the Global Counterinsurgency, clearly the conflict is viewed as persistent and ubiquitous. The global conflict is also perceived to threaten directly the national security of the United States, made explicit in policy documents from the *National Security Strategy of the United States* (2002) to the *National Military Strategic Plan for the War on Terrorism* (2006).[2] In other words, the threat requires the U.S. Government (USG) to defend the Constitution of the United States and its national interests, including its interests and allies abroad. With these assumptions in mind, the African continent, sub-Saharan Africa (SSA) in particular, has become a prominent front in the global conflict against Islamic extremists. U.S. policy in SSA faces challenges unlike previous generations because the counterterrorism

1

decisions and actions taken today will have widespread and long-lasting consequences.

SSA has never been the centerpiece of U.S. foreign and defense policy. The post-World War II focus on the Soviet Union, Europe, and East Asia largely pushed SSA to the periphery of America's strategic interests. Nevertheless, some have studied events in SSA and noted their significance to the United States since the collapse of the Soviet Union. For example, Africa scholar Dr. K. P. Magyar wrote about concerns requiring America's strategic attention, including developments in "Africa's northern tier, the Indian Ocean, the vestigial problems which remain in southern Africa, and the expanding drug traffic problems."[3] Similarly, the U.S. State Department's former top diplomat for Africa, Chester Crocker, outlined Africa's strategic importance to the United States and the West.[4] Seasoned Africa watcher Dr. Dan Henk also discussed a series of overlapping U.S. national interests in SSA, from regional stability and denial of sponsorship or safe havens for transnational threats to good governance and economic development.[5] A decade later, the research and analysis of these practitioner-scholars have risen to the attention of policymakers and military officials.

Africa in general and SSA in particular are now on the foreground of U.S. national security interests and the global conflict against Islamic extremist-terrorists (if correctly understood in a strategic context, a form of global irregular warfare[6]). The USG is now embarked on a reform of U.S. policy toward the African continent. U.S. foreign aid and assistance to SSA once promoted good governance, educational development, and better healthcare to counter global communism; today, the same foreign aid and assistance has become intertwined with U.S. efforts to counter global Islamic extremism.

Emblematic of the reorganization within the USG is the creation of a separate Department of Defense (DoD) unified combatant command for the continent, U.S. Africa Command (AFRICOM). Designed "to achieve a more stable environment in which political and economic growth can take place," AFRICOM's focus is "on war prevention rather than warfighting."[7] The focus on "war prevention" provides the USG with the rationale to develop and maintain a sustained presence in SSA that was previously unavailable. (AFRICOM and its role in U.S. counterterrorism policy is discussed later in this paper.) For better or worse, the global conflict against Islamic terrorists and their perceived threat to the United States have immersed the African continent further into U.S. counterterrorism policy.

However, before U.S. policymakers, military officers, scholars, and erstwhile experts advocate their respective policies toward SSA, it would be prudent to step back and ask the fundamental question: What is the most effective approach to U.S. counterterrorism in SSA? In other words, is the current U.S. approach to counterterrorism in SSA the most beneficial in the long term? And, if not, what is? Institutional and bureaucratic exigencies notwithstanding, these questions should be at the heart of U.S. counterterrorism policy in SSA; and they are the focus of this paper.[8]

Following this introduction, the paper is organized into three additional sections: (II) Debate in Washington; (III) Perspectives from SSA; and (IV) Summary and Recommendations. Recent examples of U.S. counterterrorism initiatives in SSA demonstrate two approaches at work, development and defense; manifestations of these approaches are the focus of Section II. At a fundamental level, the development and defense approaches are indicative of two different policy prescriptions to address the threat posed by Islamic terrorists — one requiring civilian countermeasures and the other, military. This section poses several specific questions:

1. What are the benefits of the defense approach? What are the costs?

2. What are the benefits of the development approach? What are the costs?

3. What are the metrics for success and failure? Why?

One must understand these approaches, their costs and benefits, before shifting from policy views in Washington, DC, to perspectives from SSA.

Section III provides the background for understanding the attitudes and views of terrorism and counterterrorism in SSA. Due to the geographic size of SSA and the scope of this paper, the section uses a subregional approach. It divides SSA into East, West, and Southern Africa to highlight the different geographies, histories, threats, and perceptions. East Africa includes Sudan, Eritrea, Ethiopia, Djibouti, Somalia, Kenya, Uganda, Rwanda, Burundi, Tanzania, portions of the Democratic Republic of the Congo (DRC), as well as the island nations of the Comoros and the Seychelles. West Africa includes the littoral countries from Senegal to the Republic of the Congo as well as Burkina Faso, the Central African Republic, the Democratic Republic of the Congo (DRC), Cape Verde, and Sao Tome and Principe. Southern Africa includes the DRC, Angola, Zambia, Malawi, Madagascar, Reunion, Mauritius, Mozambique, Zimbabwe, Botswana, Namibia, and South Africa. The trans-Saharan (or Sahel) countries of Mauritania, Mali, Niger, and Chad require separate attention and analysis much like the North African countries of Morocco (including Western Sahara), Algeria, Tunisia, and Libya. They will not be included in this paper. Egypt is also not included as discussion of it is better suited in a Middle East regional context.[9] With regard to each subregional perspective, this section asks:

1. How do Africans view terrorism and counterterrorism (or conflict and conflict prevention)?

2. What is the current state of civil-military and civil-law enforcement relations?

3. What, ultimately, is counterterrorism in SSA, and what does counterterrorism mean to Africans themselves?

With these subregional views, one may better comprehend the political, economic, and social views of terrorism and counterterrorism in SSA, which will benefit policymakers and military officials who focus on counterterrorism in the region.

Section IV reiterates the previous sections' major findings, and offers both thematic and specific recommendations for the USG, DoD, and the U.S. Army to answer the question: What is most effective approach for U.S. counterterrorism in SSA? Also, can and should a balance be achieved between the defense and development approaches? Based on the research and findings, the paper recommends that a new grand strategic approach to counterterrorism in SSA is needed for U.S. policy. It should focus on attaining "three standards": seizing and holding the moral high ground; winning the struggle for perceived legitimacy; and pursuing restrained counterterrorism responses. Seizing the moral high ground does not mean conducting actions better than the enemy. Rather, it means understanding what is moral in SSA

5

and striving to achieve that level of morality in all policy considerations and actions. Much like morality, legitimacy varies from one group or individual to another. U.S. counterterrorism policy must take into account the perceptions from subregion to subregion, country to country, and small folk community to small folk community. After a terrorist attack, the USG and the DoD responses are also critical. The main point of restrained counterterrorism responses is the need for unity of effort. Beyond the three standards, the USG needs to think long-term continually, build meaningful relationships in SSA, move counterterrorism beyond DoD-centric operations, and, most importantly, educate future analysts, officers, and policymakers about the African continent. What should be borne in mind throughout, and is often lost in the U.S. policymaking process, is that foreign governments and peoples (in this case, in SSA) do not always view the world according to Western liberal (especially American) values, attitudes, and beliefs. This is as true in counterterrorism policy as it is with any other strategic issue.

Before proceeding, it is necessary to clarify the theoretical perspectives, defense and development, underpinning the principal policy contentions with respect to U.S. counterterrorism policy in SSA.[10] In basic terms, development seeks "to address the root causes of terrorism," and defense focuses on "military operations to destroy terrorist targets through military strikes."[11] In this paper, the defense approach involves any and all uses of the military. The use of the military is an actualization of realist foreign policy because it is a demonstration of a nation-state's power capabilities.[12] This includes the use of the military for nonmilitary purposes, including humanitarian assistance and intervention. The defense approach in U.S. counterterrorism policy involves the use of the U.S. military as the leading instrument of national power. On the other hand, rooted in liberalist thinking, the development approach involves using nonmilitary instruments of the USG to establish peace and cooperation.[13] From humanitarian aid to financial and legal assistance to law enforcement training, USG programs not involving the military or intelligence community fall within the development approach in the paper.[14] The two theoretical approaches are further elucidated by examples in the next section, and it will become apparent that a theoretical policy divergence between defense and development exists within U.S. counterterrorism policy.

The two approaches are represented here in rudimentary fashion. The purpose is to draw a clear distinction between U.S. counterterrorism approaches being pursued in SSA. One involves use of the military; the other does not. One focuses on material power; the other, moral power.[15] It must be further emphasized that even if the military is used for humanitarian missions, this does not fall within the development approach. By definition, using the military is the defense approach. Moreover, advocates of either approach in Washington fall squarely within one of the two theoretical schools of international relations. There is no such thing as a realist-liberalist or a liberalist-realist. This is not to say, however, there is no gray theoretical area in between the two schools and approaches.[16] Rather, it is an acknowledgement that the defense and development approaches are mutually exclusive, and the two approaches dominate the mindsets of those charged with making U.S. counterterrorism policy in SSA.

II. DEBATE IN WASHINGTON

Journalist James Crawley wrote, "Africa is on the front burner with its humanitarian crises, caused by nature and man."[17] Perhaps this has always been the case, but the USG and DoD have held varying degrees of strategic interest in SSA since the end of World War II.[18] Humanitarian crises have been largely attributed to natural factors, though some have rightly pointed out that this has not always been the case.[19] The droughts and famines in 1980s brought the Horn of Africa region to the American public and Western media's attention. In the 1990s, U.S.-led United Nations (UN) intervention in Somalia and the genocide in Rwanda resulted in public outcry and dismay, also demonstrating shortcomings of U.S. strategic policy initiatives. (There is additional discussion of Somalia below.) But it took another catastrophic event, the September 11, 2001 (9/11) attacks, to enhance the perceived relevance of SSA to Washington politicians and policymakers. While 9/11 did not involve SSA directly, Afghanistan demonstrated that a failed state and ungoverned spaces could become havens and breeding grounds for Islamic extremist-terrorists; according to this thought process, nation-states in SSA have the potential to become such havens and breeding grounds.[20] Once again, the USG finds itself debating on how best to assist African nations and people. In this case, counterterrorism is the stated—and sometimes unstated—focus of engagement.

Before highlighting the development and defense approaches in practice in U.S. counterterrorism policy in SSA since 9/11, it is useful to begin with a brief overview of U.S. involvement and operations there, especially since the end of the Cold War. The pre-9/11 background in SSA is relevant to counterterrorism policy today because it reveals a general incoherence and lack of direction with regard to U.S. foreign policy in Africa. Lauren Ploch wrote informatively, "Issues on the African continent have not historically been identified as strategic priorities for the U.S. military, and U.S. military engagement in Africa has been sporadic."[21] A 1995 DoD policy document reaffirmed Ploch's assessment: "America's security interests in Africa are very limited.... [w]e see very little traditional strategic interest in Africa."[22] The 9/11 attacks may have altered the role of SSA in U.S. national security policy; nevertheless, it is useful to recall from whence it came.

SSA has been described as a "region in turmoil" since at least the African independence movements of the 1960s.[23] During the Cold War, external involvement in SSA ranged from American, Soviet, Cuban, and Communist Chinese-sponsorship of rebel movements to humanitarian UN initiatives.[24] The fall of the Berlin Wall and the demise of the Soviet Union removed much external interference in SSA, but the altered international security environment also reopened suppressed domestic and regional instabilities.[25] In the aftermath of Somalia and Rwanda, the general focus of unilateral and multilateral operations in SSA became humanitarian, peacekeeping, and peace enforcement operations, as well as training and education programs that focused on such areas as conflict resolution and civilian control of militaries. From the 1990s to today, USG initiatives have mutated from the African Crisis Response Initiative (ACRI) to the African Contingency Operations Training and Assistance program (ACOTA) and now the Global Peace Operations Initiative (GPOI).[26] These initiatives demonstrate that the United

9

States has continued to view SSA as a region in turmoil after the Cold War; however, the viewpoint did not fundamentally alter the reactive nature of U.S. policy toward the continent.

With regard to the USG presence on the continent, one of the most immediate aftermaths of the end of the Cold War was an American intelligence drawdown in SSA. In 1994, for example, it was reported that the U.S. Central Intelligence Agency (CIA) had plans to close down 15 stations in Africa due to budget constraints. In defending the proposal, one senior CIA official made the following revealing statement, "We have never been in Africa to report on Africa. . . . We went into Africa as part of the covert activity of the Cold War, to recruit (as spies) Soviet, Chinese, Eastern European, and sometimes North Korean officials under circumstances that were easier to operate under than in their home countries."[27] The post-Cold War atrophy of U.S. intelligence capabilities occurred worldwide, to be sure, but the decision to reduce the U.S. presence in Africa was a blatant acknowledgement of America's lack of strategic concern or interest on the continent. The 1994 CIA statement may be read in contrast to what Dr. Magyar wrote in 1992 when he noted, "the emergence of many new forces . . . suggests that developments in Africa have taken a new turn, which makes our close monitoring and analysis of events on that continent imperative."[28] Rather than paying closer, more detailed attention to SSA, the United States shifted resources and focus away from the continent—to the overall detriment of U.S. national security policy today.

Due to the scope of this paper, U.S. -led operations in Somalia (1992-95) will not be outlined in detail. Briefly, the U.S. -led UN Unified Task Force engaged in Operation RESTORE HOPE (December 1992 to May

1993) in response to the Somali humanitarian crisis after civil war erupted with the fall of the Siad Barre regime. U.S. forces continued participation in the UN Operation in Somalia (UNOSOM II). In October 1993, U.S. -led Task Force Ranger (composed primarily of Special Operations forces) engaged Somali militia forces in Mogadishu, which resulted in the deaths of 18 American soldiers.[29] As a result of American deaths, U.S. forces withdrew in March 1994 but later returned in February 1995 to complete withdrawal of UN forces the following month. The experience of Somalia demonstrated how U.S. military-led humanitarian missions (an early example of the potential cost of following the defense approach) may turn disastrous if political constraints hamper military operations. The failure to bring food to those in need also caused a stigma in Washington against humanitarian interventions using U.S. military forces—at least until 9/11.

Less dramatic but still noteworthy, U.S. and Kenyan forces have conducted regular training exercises known as "Edged Mallet" since 1999 along the northern coast. According to the DoD, "The exercise is designed to strengthen military-to-military relationships, increase interoperability, familiarize U.S. personnel with the environmental and operational characteristics of Kenya, demonstrate amphibious capabilities, refine and maintain operational readiness of participating forces, and promote rapport and understanding between Kenyan and U.S. personnel."[30] Since 1980 and, more recently the early 1990s, the United States has had informal military access to Kenyan facilities in exchange for military assistance.[31] The defense approach has facilitated this access to Kenya, demonstrating one of the benefits of this type approach. In addition to its military-to-military relations, the history of

U.S. engagement in Kenya — political, economic, and social — has created a sound ally for DoD in East Africa, strategically significant due to Kenya's useful position astride the western Indian Ocean as well as its support for Western interests in the region.[32]

Because of turmoil and instability, the 1990s required the U.S. military to conduct numerous noncombat evacuation missions in SSA. The list of actual and standby evacuation missions included the following countries: Liberia, Zaire (the DRC), Sierra Leone, Rwanda, Central African Republic, Gabon, and Guinea-Bissau.[33] In addition, U.S. air power was used for logistical purposes in the DRC, Sierra Leone, and Rwanda, including in support of UN missions as well as American relief and evacuation operations. Thus, U.S. operations in SSA prior to 9/11 illustrate a general lack of policy focus, sustained interest, or overall coherence. Yet, they all tended to involve or rely on the defense approach. Only marginally altered, U.S. initiatives and operations after 9/11 have followed suit.

Although nearing hyperbole, there is more truth than not in the following 2004 assertion: "Once a humanitarian concern only, [Africa] enjoys a strategic place in Washington's plans."[34] Past U.S. policies also illustrate that the once humanitarian-only focus in Africa relied on the defense approach. While the ad hoc character of operations continued, notably in the noncombat evacuation missions in Cote d'Ivoire and Liberia (2002-03), the focus of USG operations in SSA narrowed exclusively to counterterrorism. And the defense approach has remained the most favored option.

As early as January 2002, the U.S. military directed intelligence assets to conduct surveillance and reconnaissance missions over parts of Somalia. U.S. ,

British, and French aircraft were known to have taken photographs of suspected terrorist (specifically, al-Qaeda) training sites and facilities.[35] Later that year, DoD established the Combined Joint Task Force-Horn of Africa (CJTF-HOA), which arrived in the region in December and went ashore to a former French Foreign Legion outpost, Camp Lemonier, in May 2003. Nearly from the onset, CJTF-HOA operations have included humanitarian missions (infrastructure and water resource projects), medical missions (such as dental and veterinary), as well as military training missions.[36] DoD, thus, spent little time solidifying its position in the Horn of Africa for future counterterrorism missions — a tangible onset of the defense approach.

Before CJTF-HOA landed ashore, simultaneous terrorist attacks struck the Kenyan port town of Mombasa in November 2002. Al-Qaeda used a car bomb to attack the Israeli-owned Paradise Hotel (killing 18) and unsuccessfully attempted to shoot down an Israeli charter aircraft using surface-to-air missiles.[37] In the wake of the Mombasa attacks and a heightened state of security, plain-clothed U.S. Marines were deployed in May 2003 throughout the Kenyan capital of Nairobi in the vicinity of embassies and soft targets such as foreign residences and an outdoor shopping center frequented by Westerners.[38] U.S. and British Marines also conducted missions along Kenya's borders with Sudan and Somalia.[39] In this case, U.S. policy was reactive again favoring the defense approach to counterterrorism.

The United States has also created regionally focused counterterrorism programs in SSA. In West Africa, U.S. European Command (EUCOM) launched the Gulf of Guinea Guard Initiative in February 2005. The initiative aims to aid regional governments by improving maritime security off their coasts in West Africa. Under the initiative, U.S. Naval Forces Europe (U.S. NAVEUR) will assist 10 West African nations (Angola, Benin, Cameroon, Equatorial Guinea, Gabon, Ghana, Nigeria, Republic of Congo, Sao Tome and Principe, and Togo) over a 10-year period to either develop or improve their maritime security.[40] The intent is to combat drug, weapons, and people smuggling as well as illegal fishing and piracy. The initiative will focus "on and near land," initially on port security and later expand to the coastal regions inside the countries' territorial waters.[41] Directly related to the initiative, "U.S. officials [have] said that a key mission for U.S. forces would be to ensure that Nigeria's oil fields, which in the future could account for as much as 25 percent of all U.S. oil imports, are secure."[42] A parallel activity currently underway is the Africa Partnership Station (APS). Once again led by U.S. NAVEUR, APS is "designed to build maritime safety and security in Africa in a comprehensive and collaborative manner, focusing first on the Gulf of Guinea."[43] While the initiatives are designed to promote engagement and partnership, it is important to note they illustrate the defense approach in practice in SSA.

Since at least 2004, DoD has also secured agreements with several nations in West and Southern Africa to gain access to facilities.[44] These agreements encompass an array of cooperative security locations (CSLs) and forward operating sites (FOSs), and to a lesser extent, main operating bases (MOBs), in places such as Senegal, Sao Tome and Principe, Liberia, Ghana, Nigeria, Gabon, Zambia, Namibia, and South Africa.[45] The agreements allow the U.S. military access to "bare-bones" facilities for a variety of contingencies. Though similar, the distinction between CSLs and FOSs is that the latter are "warmer" facilities (i. e. , facilities with a greater number of forces rotating through and temporarily housed). MOBs, by contrast, are more permanent, with more robust infrastructure (e. g. , CJTF-HOA at Camp Lemonier).[46] "Some facilities will serve as operational hubs and house permanently stationed U.S. forces and assets. Others will allow the military to train and preposition support platforms, equipment, and supplies."[47] Having access to these sites "does help us in our engagement strategy, it does help to move places quickly," according to former EUCOM Commander-in-Chief, Marine Corps General James Jones.[48] Through its various basing arrangements, DoD has created an environment that allows for freedom of action across the continent, which shows the advantages of the defense approach to counterterrorism in SSA.[49]

Another example of the primacy of the defense approach to counterterrorism occurred in October 2005. The U.S. Agency for International Development (USAID) announced the creation of an Office of Military Affairs (OMA).[50] Intended to create an operational link between the USAID and DoD for post-conflict reconstruction and stability operations, the OMA will place senior officials within each of the five geographic unified combatant commands.[51] In addition, the OMA will serve as a point of contact for nongovernmental organizations working with the military, conduct joint exercises to add development to the planning process, and maintain an emergency response capability for future disasters and conflicts. While the December 2004 Indian Ocean tsunami and subsequent humanitarian operations were deemed a success, they also demonstrated the need for "a strategic planning relationship" between the military and the development communities.[52] Due to its newborn status, the OMA's influence on the DoD planning process is still unclear. Nevertheless, one may cogently argue that the creation of the OMA in the USAID was, in fact, a victory for DoD. The USAID may play a role in future DoD planning processes, but at the time and choosing of their hosts, the geographic combatant commands. In other words, the defense approach to counterterrorism has become the favored U.S. policy approach.

Two additional examples of DoD operations and initiatives serve to illustrate the defense trend in SSA counterterrorism policy. In December 2006, the Ethiopian military launched an intervening attack into Somalia after the Islamic Courts Union (ICU) overtook the fledgling Somali Transitional Federal Government (TFG). Perhaps unknown to the ICU, DoD has been on a quiet campaign to capture or kill al-Qaeda leaders in the Horn of Africa since the 1998 embassy bombings in Nairobi and Dar es Salaam. For several years, DoD has been training Ethiopian troops for counterterrorism operations in camps near the Somalia border, including Ethiopian Special Forces known as Agazi Commandos. According to U.S. officials, the U.S. military also used "an airstrip in eastern Ethiopia to mount airstrikes against Islamic militants in neighboring Somalia," launching two AC-130 gunship strikes on January 6 and 23, 2007.[53] Furthermore, it was reported that significant sharing of intelligence with the Ethiopian military occurred on ICU positions, including the use of American satellite information. In addition, a U.S. Special Operations unit, Task Force 88, was believed to have been deployed in Ethiopia and Kenya and ventured into Somalia.[54] While many of the details remain unclear and operations are ongoing, this direct action mission exemplifies the preeminence of the defense approach in U.S. counterterrorism in SSA.

The final example of U.S. counterterrorism in SSA is the aforementioned formation of AFRICOM, which deserves further discussion here. Announced in February 2007, AFRICOM achieved initial operating capability as a subunified command in October 2007 and is intended to achieve full operating capability (as a stand-alone command) in October 2008.[55] Much of AFRICOM's mission area will center on war prevention and a so-called "Phase Zero" strategy of engagement, which encompasses preventing conflicts at their inception using all available means such as theater security cooperation and allied capacity building.[56] With a focus on noncombat operations, AFRICOM is also slated to have a new command element known as the Directorate of Civil/Military Affairs. As envisaged, the Directorate will be the point of contact for the African Union and its standby force. In addition, it will "manage disaster relief, humanitarian assistance, and civic action projects; medical skills and health programs; security sector reform/restructuring activities; security capabilities; and command, control, and communications."[57] Despite the need (real and perceived) to reorganize the Unified Command Plan (UCP), AFRICOM was certainly and is a victory for DoD within the USG interagency process. Civilian non-DoD officials "have already expressed concern about their departments' inability to provide the number of civilian staff to the command...."[58] Civilian officials include those from the State Department and USAID; DoD has also echoed similar concern. Operationally and tactically, AFRICOM may make humanitarian operations in SSA more succinct and logistically feasible. The situation nevertheless leaves DoD as the lead strategic planning organization for counterterrorism in SSA, to the overall detriment of the development approach to counterterrorism.

Since 9/11, the United States has taken the development approach to counter terrorism only rarely. For example, South Africa and the United States signed an extradition treaty that entered into force in October 2001.[59] The agreement facilitates the transfer of criminals, including suspected terrorists, to the United States. Between 2002 and 2003, President George W. Bush also announced two programs that focused on the development approach.[60] In March 2002, Bush announced the creation of the Millennium Challenge Account (MCA); and in January 2003, the President's Emergency Plan for AIDS Relief (PEPFAR). Though not directed solely at Africa, the MCA is a USG development fund designed to reduce poverty worldwide through sustainable and accountable measures. The Millennium Challenge Corporation (MCC), the MCA administrator, uses 17 criteria to select countries for eligibility.[61] Countries in SSA with MCA "Compacts" to date include: Benin, Cape Verde, Ghana, Lesotho, Madagascar, Mali, and Mozambique.[62] Compact projects target sectors such as water, health care, and transportation infrastructure. The former Chief Executive Office of the MCC related these types of development assistance projects to promoting U.S. national security, particularly countering terrorism.[63] The PEPFAR, a multiyear, multibillion dollar USG program, works to provide prevention, treatment, and care for those with HIV/AIDS in over 100 countries worldwide. Special attention is given to 15 PEPFAR "Focus Countries," the majority of which are in SSA. These include Botswana, Cote d'Ivoire, Ethiopia, Kenya, Mozambique, Namibia, Nigeria, Rwanda, South Africa, Tanzania, Uganda, and Zambia.[64] Because of the significance of the threat posed by HIV/AIDS in SSA, it has been identified as a threat to national and international security.[65] Given the social, economic, and political environments in SSA, the MCA and the PEPFAR have direct implications on U.S. counterterrorism policy in SSA, demonstrating the development approach in practice.

In addition to the development approach's humanitarian operations, the USG has engaged in financial, legal, and law enforcement programs in SSA aimed at countering terrorism. Opened in 2001, for example, the International Law Enforcement Academy (ILEA) in Gaborone, Botswana, fosters international cooperation by supporting emerging democracies in SSA to combat crime. The Departments of State, Justice (DOJ), Homeland Security (DHS), and Treasury work in concert to implement ILEA regional seminars and specialized courses on topics such as financial crimes, counterterrorism, and border security.[66] Separate from but similar to ILEA Gaborone, the Department of Treasury's Office of Technical Assistance (OTA) has provided courses on anti-money laundering and antiterrorism financing to several SSA countries and private-sector stakeholders, including Ethiopia, Lesotho, Malawi, Namibia, Senegal, and Zambia.[67] Another example of the development approach is the DOJ's Office of Prosecutorial Development, Assistance, and Training (OPDAT) Resident Legal Advisor (RLA) in Nairobi, Kenya. Successive OPDAT RLAs in Nairobi have provided legal training and monitored legislation on counterterrorism.[68] Together, these programs demonstrate the varied character of programs that fall within the development approach.

A final example of the development approach was initiated in June 2003. The United States announced a $100 million commitment for the East Africa Counterterrorism Initiative (EACTI). EACTI provides counterterrorism equipment, training, and assistance to six countries in the region: Djibouti, Eritrea, Ethiopia, Tanzania, Uganda, and Kenya.[69] Significantly, the EACTI has also provided funds for teacher education in disadvantaged Muslim communities, greater access to education for girls, and community involvement in education. In addition, it has expanded media and information outreach as well as English language teaching.[70] But these examples of the development approach have been the exception rather than the norm.

Since 9/11, clearly the heart of U.S. counterterrorism policy in SSA has been the defense approach. This should come as no surprise as the global conflict against Islamic terrorists was couched in terms that favored the use of the U.S. military (alongside allied forces) in foreign lands. The 2002 *National Security Strategy* was explicit: "We will disrupt and destroy terrorist organizations by . . . identifying and destroying the threat before it reaches our borders. . . ."[71] The benefits of the defense approach to U.S. counterterrorism in SSA are many. First, DoD is an organization unlike any other within the USG. The resources — budget and personnel, especially — that DoD brings to bear is unmatched and therefore gives it substantial bureaucratic weight and influence within the USG interagency process. The expeditionary nature of the U.S. military naturally lends itself to tackle problems facing U.S. national interests abroad. Unlike other elements of the USG with missions abroad, moreover, the U.S. military is trained and conditioned to operate in permissive as well as hostile environments. Clearly, some exceptions exist, such as the Bureau of Diplomatic Security in the State Department. Nevertheless, the U.S. military's capabilities go a long way in dangerous social and political environments such as those in parts of SSA. Furthermore, if tasked to accomplish a mission, the U.S. military uses all available resources to accomplish that mission. While national styles may vary, all militaries around the world share this inherent mission-driven characteristic.

For all its benefits, the defense approach also has many costs when used for counterterrorism. Top among the costs of the defense approach is perception, which plays a constant role in international politics. Perception always matters, and, in certain contexts, including in countering terrorism, perception matters greatly. Because militaries are not viewed everywhere the same, use of the U.S. military abroad means different things to different people. Civil-military relations are not constant from country to country. Civil-military relations have never been and never will be the same around the world due to differences in geography, history, and culture. As a result, using the U.S. military abroad has varying implications in foreign countries and, therefore, for U.S. counterterrorism policy. Understanding unique foreign histories and cultures better enables formulation of sound U.S. military policy. The defense approach lacks substantial depth and breadth of knowledge of foreign peoples and lands, especially in SSA. This is not at all to say the U.S. military lacks the capability to gain such depth and breadth of knowledge. Rather, due to its correct focus on training and warfighting in geographic regions more directly related to U.S. strategic interests, the U.S. military does not possess institutional knowledge of SSA. Institutional means sustained, in-depth, and diverse knowledge and understanding, as opposed to narrow, temporary, and cursory. It also means possessing immediately-available subject matter expertise; this could be within the military or through the military's connections with academia and the private sector. The lack of institutional knowledge may be due to the inherent nature of the defense approach; it is a significant shortfall nonetheless.

The experiences of U.S. policy in SSA since the end of the Cold War demonstrate costs and benefits of the development approach. Such an approach to counterterrorism is beneficial because it does not involve a uniformed military presence in foreign countries. Clearly, humanitarian workers are civilians and appear less affiliated with official foreign governments. The civilian, firsthand nature of humanitarian work also creates different interpersonal relationships. Development is meant to raise the standards of living for peoples and communities. Rather than being in positions of authority, as uniformed military personnel are viewed, humanitarian workers are mostly perceived as equals—at least on the ground. Moreover, because the development approach is rooted in the civilian world, many of those who serve abroad are often educated extensively in the foreign lands, languages, peoples, and cultures across SSA. In some cases, these individuals devote their entire lives studying one particular region, country, society, or tribe. Such detailed knowledge and understanding has profound benefits for U.S. counterterrorism policy in SSA.

For all its benefits, the development approach is not without its costs. Unlike DoD, the development community is not composed of a single overarching organization, but draws on various governmental, nongovernmental, nonprofit, for-profit, and religiously-affiliated organizations and individuals. As a result, the capabilities and resources that the development approach possesses vary from country to country, region to region, and from time to time. The diversity and disunity within the development community makes some humanitarian emergencies more manageable than others. The civilian nature of the development approach also hampers efforts in hostile foreign environments, limiting the extent of development capabilities' influence as well as the very ability to conduct an operation in some cases. The development approach to counterterrorism cannot forcibly enter a foreign country to aid its people, which, in many respects, goes against its very humanitarian nature. Thus, both defense and development approaches have benefits and costs when used for counterterrorism.

With the experiences of the United States in SSA and an understanding of the costs and benefits associated with the two primary approaches to counterterrorism, what are the measurements for success and failure, and why? Metrics have been and will continue to be important to policymakers and politicians in Washington. But how does one measure the success or failure of counterterrorism policy in SSA? Raphael Perl asks a fundamentally important question for U.S. counterterrorism policymakers: "How can measurements of progress be established which are not politicized or biased [or retrospectively determined]?"[72] Perl makes a recognized assertion that the Western view is scientifically and technologically driven, thereby emphasizing the need to be able to quantify things to solve political problems. In the case of counterterrorism, the absence of attacks, the number of arrests, or the amount of money confiscated serve as measurements of success.[73] But does the opposite mean failure? This is unclear. With regard to the development approach, a common metric is dollars allocated as success and the lack thereof as failure. In addition, standard development metrics focus on quantifiable outcomes such as the number of occurrences. As is the American tendency, attempting to quantify the defense versus the development approaches leaves one comparing, for example, the frequency of attacks and arrests of suspected terrorists to the foreign aid dollars spent on a particular country or the number of individuals trained on counterterrorism finance. To what end?

For all the defense and development-related operations the USG has conducted in SSA, the precise extent to which U.S. counterterrorism policy has countered terrorism remains unclear. This ambiguity leads one back to the central question of the paper: What is the most effective approach for U.S. counterterrorism in SSA? The metrics, and lack thereof, of both defense and development counterterrorism approaches ignore at their very root the targeted region of SSA—its people, societies, and governments. Meaningful metrics for counterterrorism cannot be developed without a sound understanding of and appreciation for the perspectives across the region. Recognizing and understanding these diverse perspectives lays the foundation for sound counterterrorism policy.

III. PERSPECTIVES FROM SSA

U.S. counterterrorism does not fully account for the patterns and complexities that exist throughout SSA."Although Africa is a continent of great diversity, African states have much in common, not only their origins as colonial territories, but the similar hazards and difficulties they have faced."[74] Martin Meredith's broad historical statement is merely the starting point for understanding SSA." Nation-states in

Africa are almost all multiethnic entities in which local populations affect at best only embryonic allegiance to the nation as opposed to clan, tribe, or kin."[75] In many countries and subregions, therefore, understanding and interacting with peoples and societies may be more beneficial than doing the same with governments, which has implications for counterterrorism policy. Furthermore, "Not only is the state in Africa a nascent 'project', but also one that has become increasingly fragile in the face of the unpredictable global economic and political environment. . . ."[76] Counterterrorism policy in SSA must take the fragility of African states into consideration as well."In a number of early post-independence governments on the African continent which tended to be single-party regimes," moreover, "the military and the ruling party structures were closely intertwined at the highest level of the ruling regime (politburos/central committees)."[77] Grasping how this affects governance and individual perceptions has direct implications for U.S. counterterrorism policy.

The USG and DoD, in particular, because it already operates in the region, need a better understanding of the values and beliefs of the people in SSA if they are to formulate and execute sound counterterrorism policy.[78] C. D. Smith asks smartly: "Do we see what the Africans see? In a lot of cases, we misinterpret, we don't understand, we don't get to the heart of the issue."[79] This section is a starting point from which DoD may better interpret and understand SSA to reach the heart of the issues for U.S. counterterrorism policy. The security of the United States rests on determining the best approach; more to the point, however, the security of African nations rests on a more thorough understanding of the continent and its people. As mentioned before, each subsection represents a subregion in SSA, briefly highlighting the geographies, histories, threats, and perceptions — all of which have direct and indirect implications for sound U.S. counterterrorism policy.

West Africa.

West Africa may be characterized by "chronic armed conflict, extremely high rates of poverty, porous border security, and governmental inefficiency and corruption."[80] Though some of this characterization may be explained by indigenous human factors, geography and history have much to do with the current state of West Africa as well; therefore, they deserve brief mention.

The geography of the West African subregion, in basic terms, ranges from tropical rainforests to arid desert. The Sahara Desert defines the northern limits of West Africa's boundaries, cutting southward to affect vegetation, habitat, and local livelihood.[81] The coastal section, especially populous areas along the central portion of the Gulf of Guinea, embodies the lush tropical zone typical of the broader subregion. A variation of hills, woodland savannas, and grasslands are dispersed in between the coast and the interior. Level plains are occasionally interrupted by mountains in portions of the region. The Niger River, West Africa's longest (approximately 2,485 miles), flows from Guinea through Mali, Niger, Benin, and Nigeria, emptying into the Gulf of Guinea. Other significant rivers include the Senegal River, which flows between Senegal and Mauritania into Mali and Guinea, and the Volta River and its tributaries, which flow in Ghana, Togo, Benin, and Burkina Faso. West Africa's geography impinges directly on the people, culture, and politics of the region, all of which have an effect on terrorism and counterterrorism.

The artificial boundaries of West Africa's political map are due in large measure to the colonial heritage of the British and the French as well as the Portuguese, the Spanish, and the Germans. Briefly, the British occupied contemporary Nigeria, Ghana, Sierra Leone, the Gambia, and portions of Cameroon; the French occupied Senegal, Guinea, Cote d'Ivoire, Burkina Faso, Benin, portions of Cameroon, the Central African Republic, Gabon, and the Republic of the Congo. The British and the French pursued different colonial policies and, therefore, left local populations and political institutions in varying forms.

As in its other colonial possessions, the British objectives were primarily trade and commerce. Hand in hand with the economic features of its colonial policy, the British pursued indirect rule in West Africa, where local indigenous leaders were given a semblance of political power.[82] By contrast, the French pursued a West Africa policy of assimilation and centralization of its colonial possessions. The French "mission civilisatrice" transmitted French "civilization" and culture to its colonies, explicitly.[83] The two primary colonizers of West Africa took two very different approaches to their policies, one more heavy-handed than the other. It is necessary to bear in mind these historical legacies in the context of U.S. counterterrorism policy in the subregion.

Apart from Senegal, many West African countries have experienced numerous regime changes as a result of civil wars and coup d'états. Wars that have afflicted the subregion ranged from the civil wars in Nigeria and the Republic of the Congo in 1960s to the more recent regional wars in Liberia, Sierra Leone, and Cote d'Ivoire in the 1980s, 1990s, and 2000s. The desire to control national governments — and, therefore, natural resources and wealth — has played a seemingly unending role in the subregion's wars. In addition, tribal and religious motivations, as well as endemic corruption, contributed to the cauldron of violence, conflict, and strife in West Africa. From colonial times to the present, West Africa's history demonstrates the fractured and exploitable nature of local societies and governments. These characteristics influence the presence of nonstate threats, including terrorism.

Organized threats in the region are a result primarily of the legacy of civil wars. Local gangs and remnants of armed rebel groups exist in Liberia, Sierra Leone, and Nigeria. The presence of youth groups, gangs, and militias in the Niger Delta has been of significant concern to the USG because of their proximity to Nigeria's oil infrastructure.[84] The motivations for these attacks stem from political, social, and economic grievances — many of which are legitimate.[85] Governmental responses and corporate policy reactions have done little to alleviate local circumstances. The harbinger of 9/11 may have a presence in the subregion as well. The threat of al-Qaeda in West Africa is primarily through its use of the subregion as a financial source and transit point.[86] Notable transportation nodes include Kotoka International Airport in Accra, as well as the ports of Tema and Sekondi, all in Ghana. An example of the use of West Africa as a transit point occurred in 2005, when South African national Farhad Dockrat was detained in the Gambia for suspected terrorist activity and identified as having provided nearly $63,000 to al-Akhtar Trust, a charity that was designated in 2003 for providing support to al-Qaeda.[87] Local instability and violence, along with viable logistical hubs, make West Africa a potentially desirable region for terrorist exploitation. We now turn to perceptions in West Africa.

West Africans hold a multitude of views regarding terrorism. Given the diverse history and geography of the subregion, this should come as no surprise. For example, uneducated segments of the population relate terrorism simply with local criminal groups and robbery gangs who "terrorize" local residents. Meanwhile, educated segments of the population with greater knowledge and understanding refer to terrorism as acts perpetrated with a political bent. Educated and uneducated alike in West Africa have a general disgust for the phenomenon of terrorism and have expressed sentiments against it. Very many hate it to the core because of the bitter experiences West Africans have endured due to bloody subregional conflicts, where violence was often used against noncombatants intentionally.[88] Conflict in West Africa, then, is generally understood to open the doors for some groups to terrorize others. Other West African perspectives hold somewhat different views of terrorism. For example, from an historical point of view, some perceive terrorism as a Western European misperception of the struggle by the exploited and colonized people to gain freedom and, therefore, social opportunities.[89] Though decades have passed, experiences at the hands of the British and the French remain influential. Terrorism, according to others in West Africa, is seen as violent activities carried out by religious extremists.[90] The sectarian conflict within Nigeria is an empirical example of this view. The diversity of perspectives within West Africa regarding terrorism makes understanding counterterrorism complex and difficult.

After 9/11, many West Africans viewed intensification of counterterrorism measures as day-to-day inconveniences, particularly travelers. However, some also believe the measures are in the interests of the larger international community. Thus, many think the nature of the threat warrants the counterterrorism approach being taken.[91] Certainly, different segments of the population were exposed to counterterrorism measures in differing ways. Therefore, it is difficult to gauge the exact perceptions based on limited first-hand accounts.[92] Some in West Africa also perceive counterterrorism to be a straightforward law and order issue that requires corresponding measures reflecting this perception.[93] If counterterrorism is understood to require police and military measures, this introduces an essential aspect of local perceptions related to terrorism and counterterrorism, namely views of civil-military and civil-law enforcement relations.

Given the past prevalence of authoritarian and military regimes, many associate the military with violence and brutality. Because of differing socio-political and economic conditions, a fact of colonial history and subsequent development (and the lack thereof), fundamental differences exist with other parts of SSA in how West Africans view militaries and their relations with societies.[94] One may argue that civil-military and civil-law enforcement relations have never been positive in West Africa.[95] In many respects, a stigma remains to this day in the subregion; relations between military and security agencies and the general population remain on frosty terms.[96] According to the U.S. State Department, for example, "The populace of Nigeria distrusts the police force."[97] Thus, West African police and militaries do not garner the general support of civilian populations, who understand that militaries are meant to wage war and police, to maintain law and order.[98] Yet experiences, recent and historical, have not always demonstrated that militaries wage war and police protect the civilian population. In recent years, however, militaries have attempted to open up to the public through collaborative programs. And there has not been as much open hostility toward military or police agencies on a daily basis. Of course, lack of open hostility does not equate directly to more positive relations; but it is a beginning in the latter direction. West Africa's civil-military and civil-law enforcement relations, therefore, play a large role in counterterrorism for the subregion.

Given the subregion's history, threats, and perceptions, it is altogether unclear if the defense approach to U.S. counterterrorism is the most prudent one. While select countries within the subregion may have developed civil-military and civil-law enforcement relations (along Western lines), most have not. If the focus of U.S. counterterrorism policy is the use of the military, then this approach will inevitably run into stumbling blocks. Using the military, even for humanitarian purposes in the subregion, may hurt U.S. efforts to counter terrorism.

East Africa.

There is a saying about geography: "You can choose your friends but not your neighbors."[99] Few statements could be more apt than in the geographic and political divisions that comprise the East Africa subregion. The significance of East Africa's "geographical position along the eastern coast of Africa, on trade routes that for more than a millennium have linked South Asia with the African continent," cannot be overemphasized.[100]

Historic smuggling routes form a 2,000-mile arc from Pakistan down the eastern coast of Africa to the Comoros Islands, between Mozambique and Madagascar. According to a Western aid worker who worked in East Africa for 15 years, "They [smugglers] have been using these routes for hundreds of years, and they know every dip and cut in the coastline. Every one of them is a Muslim, and they only trust each other."[101] Maritime lines of communication facilitated the geographic spread of religion and culture from South Asia and the Persian Gulf to East Africa and beyond. (By beyond is meant Southern Africa specifically but also from East and Southern Africa to Western Europe and North America.) Between the Horn of Africa and the Arabian Peninsula, Bab el Mandeb is one of the most critical strategic choke points in the world, with a shipping lane approximately 20 miles wide (separating Djibouti and Yemen). On land, the diversity of the terrain is central to the subregional variations in climate, natural vegetation, soil composition, and settlement patterns. Notable geographic features across all of inland East Africa include highlands, plains, lowlands, grasslands, and forests (Africa's most fertile in Kenya).[102] The Great Rift Valley forms an extensive fault system bisecting large portions of inland East Africa. Other significant geographic features include the Denakil Depression near the tip of the Horn of Africa, one of the hottest places on earth; the Blue Nile River (also known as the Abay) which begins in Ethiopia and is the source of much of the water flowing into Sudan and northward to Egypt; and the lakes of the subregion, Victoria and Tanganyika, which act as important transportation pathways.

East Africa's geographic disposition and location make it an attractive subregional center of gravity in the air and sea as well as on land. For example, Nairobi's Jomo Kenyatta International Airport is a major air hub for East Africa, with regular airline services to Europe, the Middle East, and South Asia. Similarly, Addis Ababa's Bole Airport acts as a major transit point from Southeast and Southwest Asia to Africa and Europe. With a long coastline and numerous natural harbors, Kenya's port of Mombasa is one of the busiest on the east coast of Africa. Inland from the ocean, a transnational network of roads and railroads connect Mombasa with Tanzania, Uganda, and Central African countries. Finally, due to geography and a developed infrastructure, Nairobi serves as a regional banking and trade center for East, Central, and Southern Africa. East Africa's geographic position causes it to play a central role in U.S. counterterrorism policy in SSA. Moreover, the subregion's infrastructure is more economically developed than West Africa. Both East Africa's position and infrastructure, as well as its history, make it a crucial subregion for potential terrorist exploitation.

From the late 19th century, especially after the Berlin Conference of 1885, East Africa has been partitioned among European powers. From north to south, European countries with colonies in the subregion included Italy, Britain, Germany, France, and Portugal. The strategically located Horn of Africa was carved up between France, Britain, and Italy in what was then known as Somaliland (French, British, and Italian). While Germany's possessions of modern-day Burundi, Rwanda, and mainland Tanzania were cut short by its First World War loss, Britain's East Africa possessions were intended for long-term economic and commercial gain.[103] Uganda and Kenya, in particular, formed the foundation of British influence in the subregion as well as the Indian Ocean. The constant European colonial involvement in East Africa did little to abate the legacy of the historical and cultural relationship between Arabs and East African coastal peoples, however. As in the past, events in the Middle East have tended to have a spill-over effect into East Africa, largely because much of the subregion identifies with the Horn of Africa.[104] This extra-continental social identification is unique to the subregion and influences thoughts and perceptions related to terrorism.

Since much of East Africa gained independence in the 1960s, civil war and internal strife have been commonplace. An early flashpoint that continues to this day is the north-south tension in Sudan. From the onset (as early as 1955 but beginning in 1963 in earnest), southern Sudanese, mostly black and Christian-animist, have rebelled over Khartoum's "imposition of an Islamic and Arab-speaking administration."[105] To the southeast, Ethiopia's internal power struggle began in the mid-1970s, eventually culminating in a new national government and a separate Eritrea.[106] Ethiopian-Eritrean animosities exist to this day, as do the seemingly irreconcilable ethnic challenges within Ethiopian society. Since the early 1990s, Somalia's civil war and the genocidal acts in Burundi and Rwanda have been well chronicled. Less known has been the turmoil within Uganda. From the 1970s to the present, Uganda has experienced coup, dictatorship, civil war, and, now, terrorist and insurgent groups. Thus, East Africa's history over the past half-century has been one of wars of identity — over clan, tribe, ethnicity, religion, and, as always, power.[107]

The organized transnational threats within East Africa are a consequence of history and geography. All demanding a certain degree of sovereignty or feeling a sense of national grievance (some of which has been attained or alleviated), groups that pose a threat to the region include the Sudan-based Lord's Resistance Army (LRA), the Allied Democratic Forces of Uganda (ADF), and the Sudanese People's Liberation Army (SPLA).[108] In all of SSA, the threat posed by Al-Qaeda is most pronounced in East Africa. The now defunct Al-Ittihad al-Islamiya (AIAI) in Somalia has morphed into the aforementioned ICU, which maintains uncertain ties with al-Qaeda. Most recently, in late August 2007, the USG publicly announced threats to Americans in East Africa with specific reference to al-Qaeda and potential terrorist actions such as "suicide operations, bombings, kidnappings or targeting maritime vessels."[109] Thus, there is a high prevalence of terrorist and insurgent organizations in East Africa.

In addition to terrorist threats, the subregion faces problems with the illegal trafficking of goods. For example, Tanzania acts as a major arms transit country; Dabaab refugee camps in Kenya serve as illegal arms distribution centers as well. Subregional politics and conflicts have caused a proxy war between Eritrea and Ethiopia, with both countries competing for factions in Somalia. Due to internal strife and population displacement, the vast subregional Somali diaspora have developed communications and transport routes throughout the subregion. They are said to be East Africa's best black-market merchants in cars and spare parts as well as in drugs, ivory, and arms. According to one Kenyan analyst, "Somalis are everywhere. . . . If they wanted to set up a network, they could."[110] East Africa, therefore, faces much subregional turmoil — due to geography, history, and identity. How are these transnational threats viewed within the subregion?

In East Africa, like West Africa, terrorism is viewed from many different perspectives and has many different connotations. A prominent view associates terrorism with international terrorism primarily aimed against Western interests in the subregion. Along this line of thinking, East Africans perceive themselves to be drawn into a conflict foreign to and not truly associated with them.[111] Again, history and geography explain much about this perspective; but it does not prevent terrorist attacks killing East Africans. Terrorism is also viewed according to the perspective of local governments. For example, in Uganda terrorism is linked to the indiscriminate atrocities committed by the LRA. Terrorism, in this meaning, may have resonance with some of the views of terrorism in West Africa, the intentional targeting of noncombatants in particular. Another East African view of terrorism relates to broader social and economic concerns, as in the "terrorism of poverty" or the "terrorism of hunger."[112] In this broader context, terrorism is no longer related to Western interests or indiscriminate violence but rather to basic human needs. Terrorism is variously defined in East Africa, which makes countering it just as varied.

Counterterrorism is viewed with mixed perceptions and emotions in East Africa. The political context of each country tends to shape local views. In Kenya, for example, political opposition in the forms of human rights campaigners and coastal Muslims (which range from 10 to 20 percent of the total population) has prevented counterterrorism legislation from passing. The aggrieved view such measures as forms of victimization and denial of due process of law, which in turn illustrates their exclusion from political power.[113] On the other hand, in Tanzania and Uganda, counterterrorism legislation was explained to the public and passed. While the subregion has faced the more brazen and deadly al-Qaeda attacks in SSA (in 1998 and 2002), local views of counterterrorism measures have not solidified. This may be because in East Africa counterterrorism has been described as a "double-edged blade," "catalysing and supporting peace processes" while also "undermining democracy and stability."[114] In this sense, counterterrorism is both a bane and a benefit to the subregion. According to this perspective, the danger is that counterterrorism is being used in East Africa for "regime survival and state security" rather than to actually prevent terrorist attacks from occurring.[115] In general, though, the East African public has supported counterterrorism measures, especially when powers are not abused by authorities.[116] Nevertheless, there is no common view of counterterrorism within the subregion, making progress difficult to gauge.

The abuse of state power is directly related to subregional views of civil-military and civil-law enforcement relations. The relationship between militaries and the general population in East Africa is positive, so long as the former does not involve itself in law enforcement. In Kenya and Tanzania specifically, militaries enjoy very positive relations with the public as they generally confine themselves to military duties — they "stay in [their] barracks," so to speak.[117] Uganda is the exception insofar as civil-military relations are concerned. Because of domestic threats, Uganda uses its military to quell the LRA in the north as well as disarm cattle rustlers in the northeast, creating some suspicion of human rights abuse.[118] Yet Uganda is one of the more politically developed countries within the subregion. The use of the military within national boundaries strains civil-military relations in East Africa. Understanding how this affects counterterrorism is one of the subregion's biggest challenges.

The role of law enforcement in East Africa has a strong, largely negative colonial history. In many respects, the subregion is still dealing with this colonial past. Daily interactions between police and general public are on the whole stable. Difficulties sometimes arise, however, during elections when opposition parties accuse incumbent governments of police improprieties and human rights abuses. Another factor that affects the relationship between the civilian population and law enforcement in East Africa is the allegation of bribery (though one may argue this is a regular phenomenon in less-developed countries).[119] A case in point is Kenya, where the level of publicly perceived corruption is extremely high and "has come to permeate Kenyan society from bottom to top...."[120] The abuse and corruption of subregional law enforcement agencies damages civil-law enforcement relations to the overall detriment of counterterrorism efforts.

The threats and perceptions in East Africa are a direct result of its history and geography, and developing a sound understanding of them affects U.S. counterterrorism policies in the subregion. Of all the subregions in SSA, East Africa is perhaps the most strategic vis-à-vis the current conflict against Islamic extremists. The social, cultural, and economic pathways that connect East Africa to the Middle East are closely linked. In order to formulate sound policies, the USG must comprehend the ways in which these pathways affect terrorism and counterterrorism in the subregion.

Southern Africa.

The final subregion in SSA is Southern Africa. Geography has long made it a strategic location. Significant characteristics of Southern Africa include its large geographical areas, long national boundaries, and lengthy coastlines, which are difficult to patrol. Like other subregions in SSA, Southern Africa's geography varies from low-lying coastal areas and grasslands to forests and mountains. The Kalahari and Namib Deserts occupy significant portions of the subregion. In addition, major rivers that divide countries include the Orange, Limpopo, and Molopo. South Africa's geographic importance to the entire subregion cannot be overemphasized. It is the midway point on communication routes that connect South America, South and Southeast Asia, the Middle East, and Europe. Also, "South Africa has the most developed transportation, communications, and banking infrastructure in sub-Saharan Africa."[121] Although a relatively stable and open society with civil liberties, South Africa is also affected by many of the chronic social and economic problems in the region, such as high rates of poverty and unemployment. Southern Africa's geographic significance bears directly on its past colonial history.

Southern Africa's history involved many of the same European powers with interests in other parts of SSA. The Portuguese, French, German, Dutch, and British all influenced events in the subregion, centrally and on the periphery. The Portuguese were in Angola and Mozambique, the French in Madagascar and smaller Indian Ocean islands, and the Germans briefly in Namibia; the Dutch were in South Africa as were the British, who were also in Zimbabwe, Botswana,

Zambia, and Malawi. Unlike other subregions of SSA, however, one European power exerted predominant influence in Southern Africa, namely, Britain. From the coastal areas to the extreme southern portion of the subregion, Britain overtook the Dutch to gain control of all of Southern Africa, eventually expanding its influence northward to modern-day Zambia, Malawi, Zimbabwe, and Botswana. This unique colonial legacy — which encompassed social, economic, and political areas — continues to illustrate the influential role Britain holds throughout the subregion.

While tribal, ethnic, and religious sources have been the motivating factors of much violence and conflict in the two other subregions, Southern Africa's bloody history stemmed from a more basic societal distinction — race. Because of the overt policy of apartheid, the struggles of South Africa's black majority against white minority rule has earned a celebrated status and admiration throughout SSA.[122] Under white rule South Africa's "Total Onslaught" strategy aimed at disrupting the politics and economies of the black ruled "front-line states" on its borders."[123] As a result, inter- and intra-state wars occurred across the subregion: in Southern Rhodesia in 1970s, Mozambique from 1970s to 1990s, and Angola-Namibia from 1970s to 2000s. During the Cold War, foreign involvement (Cuban and Communist Chinese, especially) played a facilitating role in the subregional conflicts. While access to natural resources and control of central governments were not insignificant factors, the wars and major conflicts in Southern Africa stemmed primarily from the white-black dichotomy and its influence on society and government. This racial tension is not found in other parts of SSA, particularly given the history and publicity of the black majority's struggle.

The legacy of British colonialism has left Southern Africa with less widespread conflict and violence than the other two subregions in SSA. (This is not at all to say that crime and violence are not present in some portions of Southern Africa. Relative to West and East Africa, however, Southern Africa as a subregion is serene.) Nevertheless, Southern Africa does face threats from transnational organizations. British colonialism brought large numbers of South Asians and Muslims in general to the subregion. Islamic groups known to operate in Southern Africa include People Against Gangsterism and Drugs (PAGAD), Hamas, Hezbollah, and al-Qaeda. According to a former head of the Criminal Intelligence Unit of the South African Police Service (SAPS), South Africa is "a perfect place to cool off, regroup and plan your finances and operations. . . . The communications and infrastructure are excellent, there is a radical Muslim community, and our law enforcement is overstretched."[124] The USG concurs: "According to one reported U.S. intelligence estimate, al-Qaeda leaders are operating throughout South Africa. Other reports indicate that terrorists are exploiting the country's banking system, and that South African passports are finding their way to al-Qaeda operatives worldwide."[125] While troubled by less overall violence and instability—and, perhaps, because so—Southern Africa has become a potential haven for Islamic terrorists.[126]

Not surprising, subregional views of terrorism are rooted in its historical experiences. On the one hand, terrorism is couched in the history of the African National Congress (ANC) and the national liberation of South Africa. Often cited in the current context of terrorism and terrorists, Nelson Mandela was once labeled a terrorist with close affiliations to Yassar

Arafat and the Palestinian Liberation Organization. Furthermore, the former South African regime, with the West's support, continually labeled subregional liberation movements "terrorist organizations."[127] As a result, there is some semblance of sympathy within the subregion for current Islamic extremists. On the other hand, Islamic extremist terrorism is perceived as something that "will never" occur in Southern Africa. Some subregional analysts fear this lack of urgency and threat perception, particularly on the part of Southern Africa's political leaders.[128] A sound understanding of subregional perceptions of terrorism (and counterterrorism) must also be cognizant of the "[i]ncreased resentment by Africans of U.S. foreign policy in the Middle East [that] might further contribute to the radicalisation of ordinary people."[129] Similar to other subregions, perceptions of terrorism vary from country to country within Southern Africa. A distinction is sometimes made between domestic and international terrorism, though not always from a shared perspective. Given the colonial past, therefore, there is a fair amount of sympathy for wars of liberation, which are viewed by Southern African governments as legitimate struggles for self-determination.[130] This atmosphere of legitimacy makes the subregion a potential safe haven for terrorists. In Southern Africa, terrorism is often subsumed within the justifiable pursuit of liberation and self-determination. And these perceptions are available for terrorist exploitation.

The subregional perceptions of counterterrorism are as influenced by historical experiences as views of terrorism. Counterterrorism, as defined by the United States, is viewed with varying degrees of suspicion in Southern Africa. Even from a moderate perspective, it is seen as a means to enforce Western-centric (and, therefore, imperialist) views on the world at large and Southern Africa, in particular. Thus, a perception exists that counterterrorism of the American-led Western type is counterproductive and potentially destabilizing.[131] Such negative perceptions have ramifications throughout Southern Africa's governments and societies with regard to implementation of counterterrorism measures. Furthermore, a subregional desire is afoot to discard the politically sensitive term "counterterrorism" altogether. Instead, there is a growing desire to use broader terms like good governance, rule of law, institution building, and criminal justice reform. Southern Africa's history of liberation struggles has shaped the extent to which governments are willing to pursue counterterrorism as an end in itself and, especially, for interests perceived to be foreign to the subregion. Thus, counterterrorism in Southern Africa is perceived differently than in other subregions, and this difference has direct implications for U.S. counterterrorism policies. It should come as no surprise that subregional views of civil-military and civil-law enforcement relations are divergent as well.

Civil-military and civil-law enforcement relations are, again, a direct product of the subregion's history. As is the view of terrorism, the perceptions of civil-military and civil-law enforcement relations are variegated within Southern Africa. With regard to civil-military relations, many countries in the subregion faced the post-independence, Cold War problem of reintegrating former liberation movement armies and guerrilla groups into more formal military institutions. The successful transition to civilian-controlled militaries has varied across the subregion, but, overall, governments have done well to focus militaries on their traditional duties of defending the state.[132] The professional nature of militaries in Southern Africa stems from both European colonial history as well as decades of subregional conflict. While abuses are not nonexistent, local perceptions of militaries as agents of national liberation garner notable admiration among the civilian population.

On the other hand, Southern Africa's civil-law enforcement relations have not been as positive as civil-military relations. In South Africa, for example, the apartheid era's legacy is strong and continues to influence social relationships. During apartheid, the police and legal systems were not investigative instruments of the state but rather instruments for the control and suppression of dissident blacks. Thus, the police were not publicly respected by the majority of the population and garnered little widespread legitimacy. Though reforms have been undertaken by the SAPS, an "atmosphere of mistrust and transition" exists as "entire segments of the population remain suspicious of the police and the courts. . . ."[133] In some cases, wholesale communities believe the police are colluding with criminals and are themselves involved in criminal activity.[134] Though not as extreme a perception, in Botswana, citizens (including those in the military) hold a "somewhat contemptuous view of police capabilities."[135] This is due in large measure to the underfunding of the national police force as well as the elitist standing of the military within Botswana's society. Comparatively, civil-military relations in Southern Africa are somewhere between the more positive East African perception and the lower perceptions in West Africa. Like the other subregions, however, perceptions of civil-law enforcement relations in Southern Africa endure, negatively, the heavy hand of historical experience.

The subregion of Southern Africa is better developed politically and economically than the two other subregions. The British (as well as the Dutch) influence resulted in a degree of infrastructure development above that found in West or East Africa. At the same time, however, Southern Africa possesses historical legacies unique to the subregion, particularly apartheid and the liberation movements. These past experiences shape subregional perceptions of civil-military and civil-law enforcement relations. Southern Africa's geographic disposition and location also make it a vital strategic crossroads for Islamic extremists.

The three subregional discussions in this section are a starting point for developing a sound understanding of the lands, histories, and peoples of SSA. With this knowledge as a basis, then, what is counterterrorism in SSA and what does it mean to those in the region? Because there is no general consensus of terrorism in SSA, likewise there is no consensus view of what constitutes counterterrorism. Some view terrorism as violence directed against civilian populations, which requires more stringent enforcement of laws to establish and maintain order. Others view terrorism as a problem largely derived from the West's prejudiced and self-centered policies; this perspective would rather not involve local governments or subregional institutions with the West's so-called GWOT. History and culture speak and explain volumes about these perspectives. Moreover, identity is crucial to understanding views of both terrorism and counterterrorism. In all three subregions, local perceptions of terrorism and counterterrorism are shaped by various tribal, ethnic, religious, and racial factors. In addition to this multitude of social formations is the lasting history of European colonialism, which constantly pervades the attitudes, beliefs, and perceptions of those throughout the region. The most compelling case in point is the past relationship between terrorism and liberation struggles in SSA. Draconian government measures were used and human rights were abused in the course of countering threats labeled as "terrorism."[136] Though variegated from subregion to subregion and country to country, the blood-stained past continues to exert indeterminate amounts of influence on individuals, which have direct effects on perceptions of counterterrorism. Thus, counterterrorism means different things to different segments of the populations in SSA. There is no one agreed-upon definition, and those interacting with national and subregional governments must appreciate this singular truth.

IV. SUMMARY AND RECOMMENDATIONS

To answer the central questions of the paper (What is the best approach to U.S. counterterrorism in SSA?), the argument has been put forth that a sound understanding of SSA—its lands, histories, and people—is a key requirement. An important facet to determining the most effective approach to U.S. counterterrorism policy in SSA is the overlooked assessment and understanding of civil-military and civil-law enforcement relations. Perhaps this is because of the strong tradition of civilian rule in the West. But mirror-imagining this tradition to SSA is absolutely inexcusable. SSA militaries across subregions, with the possible exception of East Africa, have been viewed as past supporters of European colonial masters, leading to the perception today that they remain tools of oppression.[137] Militaries continue to be feared as well as loathed by the general populace, often regarded

46

as illiterate, brutal, and even drug-ridden. Also complicating the landscape, "[m]any ruling elites have used military organizations as a domestic enforcement apparatus, leading these organizations to grow and become powerful political entities."[138] Moreover, their allegiance to civilian authority is also suspect because of the frequency of extrajudicial actions taken by the military.[139]

The history of European colonialism and the authoritarian regimes that spawned in their place have also shaped subregional perceptions of law enforcement agencies. Police in SSA are less well-respected than their counterparts in the military. This negative view is due in large measure to underfunding of police agencies in comparison to military establishments.[140] More to the point, however, has been the often brutal and repressive use of the police to maintain ruling regimes and further their policies. Though militaries in SSA have been used to quell internal insurrections, police and domestic security agencies have a more soiled past, marred by violent tactics and rampant corruption. U.S. counterterrorism policies that do not fully account for SSA's civil-military and civil-law enforcement relations are inherently flawed.

SSA perceptions of terrorism and counterterrorism, civil-military and civil-law enforcement relations also suggest broader themes relevant to U.S. policy."Africans are more at ease with conflict in its multiple manifestations than their contemporaries in Europe and the United States."Adda Bozeman continued, "whereas conflict and accord, aggression and defence, and war and peace, are commonly perceived as pairs of opposites in Occidental [Western] societies, they are not experienced as mutually exclusive phenomena in Africa."[141] Terrorist attacks and counterterrorism measures in response, therefore, are not experienced as strictly opposing forces in SSA. The previous section on subregional perspectives confirms this perspective. Additional themes in SSA are the prevalence of nonliterate societies, the concept of undifferentiated time, the influence of tribalism and small folk community, and the reality of territorially fluid and ad hoc states.[142] Particularly significant is the concept of undifferentiated time, which shapes individuals to be less deadline-conscious and less linear in terms of work schedules and planning.[143] This has ramifications for the practical application of U.S. counterterrorism policy in SSA. The influence of tribalism and small folk community also leads one to disfavor authoritative controlling processes, instead favoring loyalty to lineage and family as well as religious, ethnic, and tribal groups.[144] As mentioned before, understanding the various roles of identity is crucial to formulating sound U.S. counterterrorism policies in SSA.

Taking into account the variety of subregional perspectives on terrorism, counterterrorism, civil-military and civil-law enforcement relations as well as the broader themes across SSA, in the final analysis, what is the most effective approach for U.S. counterterrorism there? Can a balance be struck between the two primary approaches, defense and development? In other words, how may the United States move forward with its counterterrorism policies in the region while fully taking into account SSA views, apprehensions, and skepticisms? Liberia's minister of information, Lawrence Bropleh, correctly pointed out in July 2007 that a secured environment attracts investors and development.[145] His statement mirrors USG policies, particularly within DoD, that development operations must in some way become synergized with defense operations; the former cannot occur without the latter.

In early 2006, DoD outlined its attempts to counter ideological support of Islamic terrorists through security, security assistance, military-to-military contacts, conduct of operations, and military information operations.[146] The growing appreciation of the development approach's importance was voiced succinctly a year later by U.S. Navy Captain Patrick Myers, director of plans and policy at CJTF-HOA. He said, "The U.S. started to realize that there's more to counterterrorism than capture-kill kinetics. Our mission is 95 percent at least civil affairs. It's trying to get at the root causes of why people want to take on the U.S."[147] Though DoD continues its mission to identify and destroy the terrorist threat beyond America's borders, the main approach focuses on defense-related development of communities and societies — this remains the defense approach because the U.S. military is the lead organization. The question, therefore, remains: Is this the most effective approach for U.S. counterterrorism policy in SSA? In the author's estimation, no.

Given the views of terrorism and counterterrorism in SSA, as well as the state of civil-military and civil-law enforcement relations, the defense approach is not the most prudent one in the long term. Moving DoD operations into the development realm (the so-called "Phase Zero" strategy) does not alter the fact that the U.S. military remains the primary organization conducting operations in SSA. This is not a balance between the two approaches; rather, it is the dominance of one over the other. In the long view, the development approach to counterterrorism in SSA is more sustainable and would have a more lasting impact. Yet, development alone will not alter manifestations of terrorism in SSA, and the approach faces extraordinary challenges when attempting to operate in hostile environments. A new approach is needed for U.S. counterterrorism policy in SSA. The paper concludes with two thematic and two specific policy recommendations.

Given the overwhelmingly divergent views of counterterrorism in SSA in contrast with those in the United States, a new grand strategic approach is necessary for U.S. counterterrorism.[148] The quantitative proclivity of the USG (DoD is not alone) to measure the effectiveness of development and defense counterterrorism operations misses the mark altogether in SSA. The United States will not be effective at countering terrorism there by simply forming AFRICOM to more efficiently conduct operations — whatever they may be. In fact, if the USG and DoD had a better comprehension of civil-military (and civil-law enforcement) relations in SSA, creating a separate unified combatant command would not have been such a priority or as publicly touted. Retrospective criticisms aside, what is needed for U.S. counterterrorism policy in SSA is (sadly, for the metrics crowd) a qualitative grand strategic approach that focuses on the following keys to effectiveness: "seize and hold the moral high ground," "win the struggle for perceived legitimacy," and pursue restrained counterterrorism responses that are "respectful of the rights and feelings even of suspect communities within the state."[149]

Given the inherent nature of the USG and DoD, it is apparent that a qualitative approach, however sound, requires some type of yard posts. Therefore, success or failure in this new grand strategic approach to U.S. counterterrorism policy in SSA should revolve around "three standards." ("Standards" are used for lack of a better term. Nevertheless, if the USG and DoD come even somewhat close to attaining them, counterterrorism policy in SSA will be for the better.)

1. **Moral high ground:** Without falling into the abyss of philosophic discourse, morality is clearly subjective (though some actions less so than others). In practical policy terms, the USG and DoD should garner a thorough understanding of SSA populations. Not only is it necessary to understand the views of public and private sector leaders, the common person on the street must be understood as well. Seizing the moral high ground does not mean conducting actions better than the enemy (a subjective endeavor, at best). Rather, it means understanding what is moral (and what is not!) in SSA and striving to achieve that level of morality in all policy considerations and actions. Holding the moral high ground, of course, requires sustained understanding and effort.

2. **Perceived legitimacy:** The thrust of the previous section on the three SSA subregions was meant to provide a cursory understanding of the multitude of perceptions in SSA. Perceptions are colored by local geographies, histories, and identities (tribal, ethnic, religious, and racial). Much like morality, legitimacy varies from one group or individual to another. What is crucial here for U.S. counterterrorism policy, then, is to understand perceptions from subregion to subregion, country to country, and small folk community to small folk community. Legitimate counterterrorism measures in the eyes of the USG or DoD will not serve a useful purpose if local perceptions are even slightly divergent. The struggle for perceived legitimacy does not occur from time to time; it is constant.

3. **Restrained responses:** Of the three standards, this one is least subjective. A terrorist attack against the

United States and its interests will likely occur again. Whether or not the USG and DoD act with violent haste (unilaterally or not) is unclear. The main point here may be as lucid as the military (and sports team) axiom—unity of effort. Unilateral USG responses may be necessary in the future; what is crucial is that the USG effort be unified. As a 2006 U.S. Senate Foreign Relations Committee report rightly noted, "one misstep or poorly calculated military or other operation can significantly set back the full range of U.S. counterterrorism efforts in an entire region."[150] In SSA, such a fatal move could affect one country, one or more subregions, or the entire continent. Therefore, U.S. counterterrorism players and policies need to be on the same page. AFRICOM may assist in attaining this standard, but it must be remembered that DoD is only one of many USG departments and agencies operating in the vast expanse of SSA.

All three standards point to another thematic recommendation for U.S. counterterrorism policy in the region: Think long term and build relationships. Though simplistic, this thematic recommendation is difficult to pursue throughout the USG. It is, therefore, heartening that progress is being made on these lines within DoD. For example, Rear Admiral Robert Moeller, executive director of the AFRICOM Transition Team, said in June 2007, ". . . it's important that our African partners see a consistency in our approach. Whether that's a long-term presence, like CJTF-HOA, or rotational, our engagement needs to be sustained."[151] Such growing appreciation for the long-term and interactive nature necessary for successful U.S. counterterrorism policy in SSA was further voiced by Major David Malakoff, director of public affairs at CJTF-HOA. He pondered, "How much of a difference are we going to make? That's hard to say. It's not something that we can judge short-term. Our target group is today's children, so we're not going to know for 10 or 15 years. But we hope that, in the long run, we could be saving lives."[152] In the long view, also, the USG should consider seriously an overhaul of civilian departments and agencies operating abroad (especially the Departments of State, Justice, and Homeland Security) so they become more joint and unified. Much as the Goldwater-Nichols Act (1986) reorganized DoD, all civilian USG departments and agencies with foreign activities and operations need massive reform to meet 21st century challenges and anticipate opportunities. To conduct successful counterterrorism in SSA (and around the world), the USG as a whole needs to become better streamlined and more cohesive.[153] The general thematic recommendation here is already being appreciated. Nevertheless, the USG and DoD would benefit from a constant refrain of *think long term, build relationships, think long term, build relationships*. And it must be remembered that progress will be "slow and organic, and measured subjectively in successive layers of trust."[154] Building long-term relationships should be a persistent theme for U.S. counterterrorism policy in SSA.

The first specific policy recommendation may not be well-received, but it is necessary to do for effective counterterrorism: U.S. counterterrorism in SSA must move beyond the singular confines of DoD operations. A more comprehensive, grand strategic approach is necessary to achieve the standards of the moral high ground, perceived legitimacy, and restrained counterterrorism responses. It is certainly true that "[t]rends in international cooperation are important in measuring [long-term] progress against terrorism."[155]

Nevertheless, the search for cooperation is not a strategy in itself for effective counterterrorism policy in SSA (or for any other strategic policy for that matter). Close DoD consultations with SSA countries alone, which may promote mutual exchange of interests and foster closer alliances, will not achieve the key standards for successful counterterrorism in SSA. Instead what is meant by this specific recommendation is more nuanced. DoD lead is acceptable, for now. More regular and routine humanitarian and civil affairs operations may continue apace, and they appear now to be occurring or are in train. For example, acronyms such as COMREL (community relations), MEDCAP (medical civic action program), and VETCAP (veterinary civic action program) are more frequently used in the lexicon of DoD in SSA. But the defense approach cannot be sustained indefinitely, nor should it be for counterterrorism policy in SSA. Disaster relief and humanitarian assistance packages in themselves will not counter terrorism directed against the United States and its interests.[156] For successful counterterrorism in the long term, more USG participation outside of the military domain is essential, particularly in fields of public communications, education, law enforcement, and legal affairs. Clearly, the basic human conditions and civil societies in SSA must be improved as well, and the entire USG may play a larger role to assist in this endeavor.[157] While nonprofit and nongovernmental organizations may act in ways beneficial to the United States, successful counterterrorism policy in SSA requires appropriate department and agency involvement from the entire USG.

Much of current and future USG activities in SSA will be for naught if the entire region is not well-understood — geographically, historically, and culturally. The second specific recommendation is to educate, educate, educate. Smartly, two U.S. Army officers wrote, "One fallacy shared by Americans and many Westerners is the belief that civic action projects are always positive and relatively simple to execute. The idea that local populations must perceive such activities as beneficial is just not true."[158] All across SSA, local populations have thoughts and perceptions that are different from Americans and Westerners, in general. USG activities must recognize these differences and formulate prudent policies accordingly. Moreover, a U.S. embassy official in West Africa asserted, "Since African security organizations do not always mirror the states they serve, Washington can no longer operate on the assumption that providing security assistance to African military and police organizations will automatically increase their professionalism and support of democratic institutions."[159] Therefore, there is a dire need for the greater study of SSA at U.S. professional military education institutions and, perhaps, more importantly, at American institutions of higher learning. Leaders must learn early and often about the cultures, traditions, and diverse African approaches. DoD and USG elements operating in SSA should engage in "nuanced research and analysis of history, politics, and culture . . . in particular of their leadership and strategic culture."[160] Part and parcel of education are firsthand experiences. Thus, more exchange visits to SSA across the board are needed: professional military, civilian government, and higher education. Likewise, there should be more regular and routine personal contact and communication with peoples and governments, keeping in mind interactions are necessary with local populations, individual countries, and subregional institutions. Through the entire educational process, the key to achieving the standards for effective counterterrorism in SSA should be an emphasis on the quality of education and interactions rather than the quantity. One meaningful visit means much more than 10 terse PowerPoint-driven briefings.

With greater knowledge, understanding, and appreciation of SSA and its subregions, DoD (and all other USG elements operating in the region) may then be frank about U.S. interests, concerns, and desires—some of which may not coincide with SSA governments and people. For counterterrorism policy and other strategic issues, the differences must be understood and mutually known. Indeed, it could be that one overarching U.S. counterterrorism policy for SSA is entirely inappropriate. After all, "There are many African countries; the United States accordingly needs many different African policies."[161] Whatever the case may be, the USG and DoD must recognize that Africans have different perspectives, approaches, and, therefore, solutions. The United States needs to identify the various tribal, ethnic, and religious forces and how they influence social, political, and economic life throughout SSA. To use "the iceberg metaphor," the United States needs to learn about "the hidden elements of local cultures," "the expanse of culture that exists below the surface of the immediate perception."[162] In addition, DoD and the USG in general must appreciate that, at the end of the day, "the true solutions to the dilemmas facing sub-Saharan Africa [including terrorism] must come from within."[163] Understanding America's limitations in SSA requires innovative policy thinking and agility. For example, one may ask, what can Americans learn from Africa?[164] Or, as Air Force Colonel (Dr.) Victor Folarin, a Nigerian-American physician with the EUCOM Medical Readiness Office said, "Do not give Africans fish, teach them how to fish instead."[165]

Finally, to attain the three standards of the grand strategic approach to U.S. counterterrorism policy in SSA requires a generation of officers, analysts, and, above all, students. DoD should prepare to develop future generations whose interest in SSA matches their knowledge and understanding. Without a doubt, this is necessary for the sake of sound counterterrorism policy as well as future foreign and military policies in SSA. And, given the long history of foreign area study, the U.S. Army is an appropriate institution to begin this inculcation.

ENDNOTES

1. Former Labour P.M. Callaghan quoted from William J. Foltz, "Africa in Great-Power Strategy," in William J. Foltz and Henry S. Bienen, eds., *Arms and the African: Military Influences on Africa's International Relations*, New Haven, CT: Yale University Press, 1985, p. 1.

2. George W. Bush, *The National Security Strategy of the United States of America*, Washington, DC: The White House, September 2002, and Chairman of the Joint Chiefs of Staff, *National Military Strategic Plan for the War on Terrorism*, Washington, DC: Department of Defense, February 2006.

3. K. P. Magyar, *Africa's Realignment and America's Strategic Interests in the Postcontainment Era*, Maxwell Air Force Base, AL: Air University Press, February 1992, p. 25. Dr. Magyar was especially prescient when he wrote, "Africa is being systematically divided between Arabs and Muslims on one side and black Africans and non-Muslims on the other. This portends the establishment of a dividing line between Mauritania and Senegal, through Mali, Chad, and Sudan and between Somalia and Kenya on the Indian Ocean." *Ibid.*, p. 16.

4. Chester A. Crocker, "Why Africa is Important," *Foreign Service Journal*, Vol. 72, No. 6, June 1995, pp. 24-33. Crocker served as Assistant Secretary of State for African Affairs from 1981 to 1987.

5. Strikingly similar to current U.S. Africa policy, Henk explained in "US National Interests in Sub-Saharan Africa," *Parameters*, Vol. XXVII, No. 4, Winter 1997-98, pp. 92-107. Colonel Henk (U.S. Army, Ret.) served as an African Foreign Area Officer and an Army attaché in four African countries.

6. For a commanding elucidation of irregular warfare and the American strategic context, see Colin S. Gray, *Irregular Enemies and the Essence of Strategy: Can the American Way of War Adapt?* Carlisle, PA: Strategic Studies Institute, U.S. Army War College, March 2006.

7. U.S. Africa Command, "About AFRICOM," no date; available from *www.africom.mil/AboutAFRICOM.asp*, accessed October 25, 2007. In theory, everything short of war may be classified as "war prevention." Because this paper is not a theoretical examination of DoD policy, suffice it to say here that AFRICOM has quite a broad mission on the continent.

8. The research end date for the paper was November 18, 2007.

9. Egypt is not a part of AFRICOM, which confirms my approach.

10. Diplomacy is a third "D" outlined in U.S. national security strategies. But from a strategic perspective, diplomacy is part and parcel of development; the latter cannot exist without the former. Moreover, those who tend to advocate diplomacy are the same as those who advocate development, and vice versa. Of course, this is not so clear-cut in U.S. policy documents, particularly when terms such as "transformational" are added to diplomacy. See for example, George W. Bush, *The National Security Strategy of the United States of America*, Washington, DC: The White House, March 2006, pp. 33, 44-45.

11. Lauren Ploch, *Africa Command: U.S. Strategic Interests and the Role of the U.S. Military in Africa*, CRS Report for Congress, RL34003, Washington, DC, July 6, 2007, p. 17. Ploch also notes an "increasing emphasis on Information Operations (IO) in Africa, which use information to improve the security environment and

counter extremist ideology through military information support teams deployed to U.S. embassies. "It is debatable the extent to which information may improve physical security; nevertheless, these types of operations are more defense than development, especially if managed and run by military personnel.

12. For a concise selection of realist thinkers, see Richard K. Betts, ed., *Conflict After the Cold War: Arguments on Causes of War and Peace*, 3rd ed., New York: Pearson Longman, 2008, pp. 53-117.

13. For a concise selection of liberalist thinkers, see *Ibid.*, pp. 119-167.

14. Because the intelligence community by and large supports the military (or is the basis for military action), it is grouped into the defense approach.

15. Betts, p. 465.

16. One could argue that the constructivist school of international relations is gaining ground since it spawned in the 1990s. For readings in this school, see *Ibid.*, pp. 195-264. Discussion of this school within the present context is beyond the scope of the paper, and it remains to be seen how relevant constructivism will be decades hence.

17. James W. Crawley, "Washington Date Line: Africa commands new Pentagon attention," Media General News Service, June 6, 2007; available from *washdateline.mgnetwork.com/ index.cfm?SiteID=wsh&PackageID=46&fuseaction=article.main&Art icleID=9499&GroupID=181*, accessed June 6, 2007.

18. The North Africa campaigns of World War II have received their due attention. However, from a strategic history perspective, it would be most useful to study World War I campaigns in East and West Africa. For a start, see Charles Hordern, *Military Operations, East Africa, Volume I, 1914-1916*, Nashville, TN: Battery Press, 1990; and F. J. Moberly, *Military Operations, Togoland & the Cameroons*, Nashville, TN: Battery Press, 1995.

19. For a detailed account of the strategic use of famine and starvation by armed forces for national policies, see Robert D. Kaplan, *Surrender or Starve: Travels in Ethiopia, Sudan, Somalia, and Eritrea*, New York: Vintage Books, 2003.

20. For a DoD perspective, see Theresa Whelan, "Ungoverned Spaces: A New Threat Paradigm," *Rethinking the Future Nature of Competition and Conflict Seminar Series*, Johns Hopkins University Applied Physics Lab, Arlington, VA, December 19, 2005.

21. Ploch, p. 11.

22. Office of International Security Affairs, U.S. Department of Defense, *U.S. Security Strategy for Sub-Saharan Africa*, Washington, DC, August 1, 1995; available from *www.defenselink.mil/speeches/ speech.aspx?speechid=943*, accessed November 18, 2007.

23. See Anthony K. Crawford, *The Search For Stability in Sub-Saharan Africa – An American Perspective*, Fort Leavenworth, KS: School of Advanced Military Studies, U.S. Army Command and General Staff College, May 1998.

24. For an oft-overlooked example of Communist Chinese involvement, see Donovan C. Chau, "Assistance of a Different Kind: Chinese Political Warfare, 1958-1966," *Comparative Strategy*, Vol. 26, No. 2, April-June 2007, pp. 141-161.

25. The big exception, of course, has been the Chinese. See Donovan C. Chau, *Political Warfare in Sub-Saharan Africa: U.S. Capabilities and Chinese Operations in Ethiopia, Kenya, Nigeria, and South Africa*, Carlisle, PA: Strategic Studies Institute, U.S. Army War College, March 2007.

26. For a background, see Nina M. Serafino, *The Global Peace Operations Initiative: Background and Issues for Congress*, CRS Report for Congress, RL32773, Washington, DC, June 11, 2007.

27. Walter Pincus, "CIA Plans to Close 15 Stations in African Pullback," *Washington Post*, June 23, 1994, p. A20.

28. Magyar, p. 26.

29. For a first-rate account, see Mark Bowden, *Black Hawk Down: A Story of Modern War*, New York: Atlantic Monthly Press, 1999.

30. Office of the Assistant Secretary of Defense (Public Affairs), "Exercise Edged Mallet 99 Announced," *News Release*, No. 040-99, January 29, 1999, available from *www.defenselink.mil/releases/release.aspxreleaseid=1966*, accessed November 9, 2007.

31. In the 1980s, Kenya was used to support commitments in the Indian Ocean; in the 1990s, operations in Somalia. Federal Research Division, *Country Profile: Kenya*, Washington, DC: Library of Congress, June 2007, p. 20; and Ploch, p. 8.

32. A new scholarly work on U.S. -Kenyan strategic relations is necessary.

33. For more, see Ploch, p. 30-31.

34. Stewart M. Powell, "Swamp of Terror in the Sahara," *Air Force Magazine*, Vol. 87, No. 11, November 2004, p. 52.

35. Thomas E. Ricks, "Allies Step Up Somalia Watch," *Washington Post*, January 4, 2002, p. A01.

36. For more, see Combined Joint Task Force-Horn of Africa, U.S. Central Command, *Fact Sheet*, October 2007, available from *www. hoa. centcom. mil/factsheet. asp*, accessed November 13, 2007.

37. To date, there has not been a detailed, scholarly account of the November 2002 Mombasa attacks and subsequent counter-terrorism operations.

38. Emily Wax, "Marines Comb Borders As Worries Rise in Kenya," *Washington Post*, May 17, 2003, p. A17.

39. Little public information is known regarding these operations. *Ibid*.

40. Andrew Feickert, *U.S. Military Operations in the Global War on Terrorism: Afghanistan, Africa, the Philippines, and Colombia*, CRS

Report for Congress, RL32758, Washington, DC, August 26, 2005, p. 14.

41. *Ibid.*

42. Greg Jaffe, "In Massive Shift, U.S. Is Planning To Cut Size of Military in Germany," *Wall Street Journal*, June 10, 2003, p. A1.

43. U.S. Naval Forces Europe-U.S. Sixth Fleet, *Africa Partnership Station: An Initiative to Promote Maritime Safety and Security*, White Paper, October 21, 2007, p. 6.

44. With regard to East Africa, as aforementioned the DoD has had access to facilities in Kenya since the 1990s and Camp Lemonier in Djibouti since 2003. Since then, DoD facilities have propped up in strategically significant Uganda as well as Ethiopia. Powell, p. 54.

45. Also places in Mauritania, Mali, Niger, and Chad, though these are outside the scope of this paper. Countries identified among Ploch, p. 8; Herbert Docena, *'At the Door of All the East': The Philippines in United States Military Strategy*, Special Report No. 2, Quezon City, Philippines: Focus on the Global South, November 2007, pp. 9, 11, 13; and Peter Kagwanja, "Global Cop USA Seeks More Presence in Africa," *Nation (Nairobi)*, July 20, 2007, available from *allafrica.com/stories/200707200404.html*, accessed August 7, 2007.

46. Compare specific definitions in Chairman of the Joint Chiefs of Staff, *Department of Defense Dictionary of Military and Associated Terms*, Joint Publication 1-02, Washington, DC: U.S. Government Printing Office, October 17, 2007, pp. 124, 217, and 322.

47. John T. Bennett, "Jones: U.S. has 'security locations' deals with up to 10 African nations," *Inside the Pentagon*, October 27, 2005.

48. *Ibid.*

49. On the one hand "freedom of action" refers to a "new term" for jumping-off points from smaller outposts around the

world in the DoD's 2004 *Global Posture Review*. "Pentagon Expands Bases In Little-Known Places," *USA Today*, September 23, 2004, p. 5. On the other hand, the author was privileged to hear the term as early as 1998 from Dr. Harold W. Rood at Claremont McKenna College.

50. U.S. Agency for International Development, *USAID-DoD Relations*, briefing at Public Meeting of Advisory Committee on Voluntary Foreign Aid, Washington, DC, October 19, 2005.

51. The geographic unified combatant commands include Northern, Southern, European, Central, and Pacific. One may also envision placement of senior USAID officials in the emerging Africa Command.

52. Todd Bullock, "USAID Announces New Office of Military Affairs," *Washington File*, October 24, 2005, available from *usinfo. state.gov/xarchives/display.html?p=washfile-english&y=2005&m=October&x=20051024152233TJkcolluB0.4715998*, accessed November 3, 2007.

53. Michael R. Gordon and Mark Mazzetti, "U.S. Used Base in Ethiopia to Hunt Al Qaeda in Africa," *New York Times*, February 23, 2007, p. A1.

54. *Ibid.*

55. President Bush reportedly made the decision for AFRICOM in December 2006. Ploch, p. 1, footnote 2.

56. Charles F. Wald, "The Phase Zero Campaign," *Joint Forces Quarterly*, Issue 43, 4th Quarter 2006, pp. 72-75. General Wald (U.S. Air Force) was formerly Deputy Commander of EUCOM, traditionally the top DoD position overseeing the African continent. For an elucidation of theater security cooperation, see Clarence J. Bouchat, *An Introduction to Theater Strategy and Regional Security*, Carlisle, PA: Strategic Studies Institute, U.S. Army War College, August 2007.

57. Ploch, p. 8.

58. *Ibid.*, p. 23.

59. Ted Dagne, *Africa and the War on Terrorism,* CRS Report for Congress, RL31247, Washington, DC, January 17, 2002, p. 2.

60. Though not explicitly so from the onset.

61. Criteria result in scores ranging from low (that may obtain Threshold Assistance) to high (that may engage in a Compact Agreement).

62. The Gambia also had an MCA compact but it was suspended in June 2006. Millennium Challenge Corporation, "Countries: The Gambia," no date, available from *www.mcc.gov/countries/gambia/index.php*, accessed November 15, 2007.

63. Paul Applegarth, "The Millennium Challenge Corporation's Global Impact," Testimony Before the Senate Committee on Foreign Relations, Washington, DC, April 26, 2005.

64. For more detailed information, see The United States President's Emergency Plan for AIDS Relief, "Focus Countries," no date, *www.pepfar.gov/countries/c19418.htm*.

65. Mark Dybul, "PEPFAR: An Assessment of Progress and Challenges," Testimony Before the House Committee on International Relations, Washington, DC, April 24, 2007.

66. Bureau for International Narcotics and Law Enforcement Affairs, *International Narcotics Control Strategy Report, Vol. II,* Washington, DC: Department of State, March 2007, p. 11.

67. *Ibid.*, p. 28.

68. *Ibid.*, p. 25.

69. William P. Pope, "Eliminating Terrorist Sanctuaries: The Role of Security Assistance," Testimony Before the House Committee on International Relations, Subcommittee on International Terrorism and Nonproliferation, Washington, DC, March 10, 2005.

70. Office of the Coordinator for Counterterrorism, U.S. Department of State, *Country Reports on Terrorism 2004*, Washington, DC, April 2005, p. 29.

71. George W. Bush, *The National Security Strategy of the United States of America*, p. 6.

72. Raphael Perl, *Combating Terrorism: The Challenge of Measuring Effectiveness*, CRS Report for Congress, RL33160, Washington, DC, March 12, 2007, p. 9.

73. *Ibid.*, p. 10.

74. Martin Meredith, *The Fate of Africa: A History of Fifty Years of Independence*, New York: Public Affairs, 2005, p. 14.

75. LaVerle Berry, Glenn E. Curtis, *et al.*, *Nations Hospitable to Organized Crime and Terrorism*, Washington, DC: Federal Research Division, Library of Congress, October 2003, p. 3.

76. Naison Ngoma, "Civil-Military Relations in Africa: Navigating Uncharted Waters," *African Security Review*, Vol. 15, No. 4, December 1, 2006, p. 99.

77. *Ibid.*, p. 108.

78. The Department of National Security and Strategy at the U.S. Army War College has begun using an Analytical Cultural Framework in select area studies courses. I thank Lieutenant Colonel (U.S. Air Force) Clarence J. Bouchat for bringing this to my attention.

79. C. D. Smith, from the Defense Department's African Center for Strategic Studies, quoted in Charlie Coon, "AFRICOM struggles to improve image of U.S.," *Stars and Stripes (Mideast Edition)*, July 10, 2007, available from *www.estripes.com/article. asp?section=104&article=47246*, accessed July 10, 2007.

80. Berry, Curtis, *et al.*, p. 27.

81. Again, the trans-Saharan countries of Mauritania, Mali, Niger, and Chad are best discussed separately.

82. Indirect rule's strongest advocate was Frederick D. Lugard. For example, see his book, *The Dual Mandate in British Tropical Africa*, London: W. Blackwood and Sons, 1922.

83. See L. Gray Cowan, "The New Face of Algeria: Part I," *Political Science Quarterly*, Vol. 66, No. 3, September 1951, pp. 340-356, for a description.

84. Email correspondence by author with State Department official stationed at U.S. Consulate General, Lagos, Nigeria, March 9, 2006.

85. An excellent overview is International Crisis Group, *The Swamps of Insurgency: Nigeria's Delta Unrest*, Africa Report No. 115, Dakar/Brussels, August 3, 2006.

86. For a compelling examination, see Douglas Farah, *Blood from Stones: The Secret Financial Network of Terror*, New York: Broadway Books, 2004.

87. Jonathan Schanzer, "Pretoria Unguarded: Terrorists Take Refuge in South Africa," *Weekly Standard*, Vol. 12, No. 35, May 28, 2007.

88. Email correspondence by author with West African nongovernmental organization researcher, August 2, 2007.

89. Email correspondence by author with Dr. Gani Yoroms, African Centre for Strategic Research and Training, National War College, Nigeria, August 1, 2007.

90. Email correspondence by author with Dr. Istifanus Zabadi, African Centre for Strategic Research and Training, National War College, Nigeria, August 4, 2007.

91. Email correspondence by author with West African nongovernmental organization researcher.

92. This is a methodological problem that affects most analytical assessments of local perceptions.

93. Email correspondence by author with Dr. Istifanus Zabadi.

94. See, for example, T. S. Cox, *Civil-Military Relations in Sierra Leone: A Case Study of African Soldiers in Politics*, Cambridge, MA: Harvard University Press, 1976.

95. Email correspondence by author with Dr. Istifanus Zabadi.

96. Email correspondence by author with Dr. Gani Yoroms.

97. U.S. Department of State's *International Narcotics Control Strategy Report 2003*, cited in Berry, Curtis, *et al.*, p. 28.

98. Email correspondence by author with West African nongovernmental organization researcher.

99. Well-known to the author, but relayed to him again during interview conducted by author with senior Kenyan embassy official at Embassy of Kenya, Washington, DC, August 24, 2007.

100. Berry, Curtis, *et al.*, p. 9.

101. Dexter Filkins with Marc Lacey, "Kenya's Porous Border Lies Open to Arms Smugglers," *New York Times*, December 4, 2002, p. A18.

102. Federal Research Division, p. 5.

103. And, according to some, the British never intended to leave Kenya. Interview conducted by author with senior Kenyan embassy official.

104. *Ibid.*

105. Federal Research Division, *Country Profile: Sudan*, Washington, DC: Library of Congress, December 2004, p. 3.

106. A thorough account of the former is found in John Young, *Peasant Revolution in Ethiopia: The Tigray People's Liberation Front, 1975-1991*, New York: Cambridge University Press, 2006.

107. A truly fascinating and necessary study is a strategic history of the East Africa subregion.

108. Though dated and not all-inclusive, Christopher S. Clapham, ed., *African Guerrillas*, Bloomington: Indiana University Press, 1998, is useful.

109. Overseas Security Advisory Council, "Public Announcement: East Africa," *Consular Affairs Bulletins*, August 31, 2007, available from *www.osac.gov/Reports/report.cfm?contentID=72989*, accessed September 27, 2007.

110. Moustapha Hassouna, a professor of security studies at the University of Nairobi, quoted in Danna Harman, "Why Radicals Find Fertile Ground in Moderate Kenya," *Christian Science Monitor*, December 6, 2002, p. 7.

111. Email correspondence by author with senior Tanzania police official, August 4, 2007.

112. Interview conducted by author with senior Kenyan embassy official.

113. Federal Research Division, *Country Profile: Kenya*, p. 4.

114. View espoused by prominent subregional scholar Peter Kagwanja, "Counter-terrorism in the Horn of Africa: New Security Frontiers, Old Strategies," *African Security Review*, Vol. 15, No. 3, August 1, 2006, pp. 72 and 84.

115. *Ibid.*, p. 84.

116. Email correspondence by author with senior Tanzania police official.

117. Interview conducted by author with senior Kenyan embassy official.

118. Email correspondence by author with senior Tanzania police official.

119. *Ibid.*

120. Transparency International ranked Kenya 84th out of 91 in a survey on publicly perceived corruption in June 2001. Survey cited from Berry, Curtis, *et al.*, p. 17.

121. *Ibid.*, p. 23.

122. For a moving firsthand account, see Nelson Mandela, *Long Walk to Freedom: The Autobiography of Nelson Mandela*, Boston: Little, Brown, 1994.

123. Foreign and Commonwealth Office, United Kingdom, "Country Profile: Mozambique," *Countries and Regions*, October 23, 2007, available from *www.fco.gov.uk/servlet/ Front?pagename=OpenMarket/Xcelerate/ShowPage&c=Page&cid=1 007029394365&a=KCountryProfile&aid=1019744977697*, accessed October 30, 2007.

124. Gideon Jones quoted in Robert Block, "In South Africa, Mounting Evidence of al Qaeda Links," *Wall Street Journal*, December 10, 2002, p. A1.

125. Schanzer.

126. Kurt Schillinger, "Al-Qaida in Southern Africa: The Emergence of a New Front in the War on Terror," *Armed Forces Journal*, No. 143, No. 7, February 2006, pp. 12-16, is useful.

127. Email correspondence by author with South African nongovernmental organization worker, April 20, 2007.

128. Anneli Botha, "South Africa and the 'War Against Terrorism'," Centre for International Political Studies, University of Pretoria, Electronic Briefing Paper, No. 29, 2007, available from *www.cips.up.ac.za/files/pdf/ebriefing/29-2007_South_Africa_and_the_ War_against_Terrorism_by_Anneli_Botha.pdf.*

129. *Ibid.*

130. Email correspondence by author with South African nongovernmental organization worker, July 12, 2007.

131. *Ibid.*

132. Two interesting works using different theoretical models are Thomas H. Burchert, "From Apartheid to Democracy: The Civil-Military Relations in the Republic of South Africa," M. A. thesis, Naval Postgraduate School, June 2004; and Jessica Schafer, *Soldiers at Peace: Veterans of the Civil War in Mozambique*, New York: Palgrave Macmillan, 2007.

133. Berry, Curtis, *et al.*, p. 26.

134. Email correspondence by author with South African nongovernmental organization worker, July 12, 2007.

135. Dan Henk, "The Botswana Defense Force: Evolution of a Professional African Military, *African Security Review*, Vol. 13, No. 4, December 1, 2004, p. 93.

136. Email correspondence by author with South African nongovernmental organization worker, April 20, 2007, and Gani Yoroms, "Defining and Mapping Threats of Terrorism in Africa," in Wafula Okumu and Anneli Botha, eds., *Understanding Terrorism in Africa: In Search for an African Voice*, Pretoria: Institute for Security Studies, 2007, p. 3.

137. Benjamin Mibenge, "Civil-Military Relations in Zambia: A View from the Military," in Gilbert Chileshe, Margaret Chimanse, Naison Ngoma, Paul Lwando, and Tasila Mbewe, eds., *Civil-Military Relations in Zambia: A Review of Zambia's Contemporary CMR History and Challenges of Disarmament, Demobilisation and Reintegration*, Pretoria: Institute for Security Studies, August 1, 2004, pp. 33-34.

138. Office of International Security Affairs.

139. Ngoma, p. 102.

140. For example, Alice Hills, *Policing Africa: Internal Security and the Limits of Liberalization*, Boulder, CO: Lynne Rienner, 2000.

141. Adda B. Bozeman, *Conflict in Africa: Concepts and Realities*, Princeton: Princeton University Press, 1976, p. 370.

142. All are explained masterfully in *Ibid.*, especially pp. 69-146.

143. Henri Boré, "Cultural Awareness and Irregular Warfare: French Army Experience in Africa," *Military Review*, July-August 2006, p. 109.

144. *Ibid.*, pp. 109, 111.

145. James Butty, "Liberia Lobbies for AFRICOM Headquarters," *Voice of America*, July 6, 2007, available from *www. voanews. com/english/Africa/2007-07-06-voa3. cfm*, accessed July 10, 2007.

146. Chairman of the Joint Chiefs of Staff, *National Military Strategic Plan for the War on Terrorism*, pp. 24-27.

147. Nicholas D. Kristof, "Aid Workers With Guns," *New York Times*, March 4, 2007, p. A13.

148. Grand strategy is defined as "the calculated and coordinated use of all the resources of a state or nonstate actor to preserve and enhance long-term interests." Donovan C. Chau, "Grand Strategy into Africa: Communist China's Use of Political Warfare, 1955-1976," Ph.D. dissertation, University of Reading, 2005, p. 3.

149. Colin S. Gray, *War, Peace and International Relations*, New York: Routledge, 2007, pp. 255-257. Though specific to psychological operations, Dr. Jerrold Post mirrors the intent of Dr. Gray when he identifies four major elements of counterterrorism as: inhibiting potential terrorists from joining terrorist groups, producing dissention within groups, facilitating exit from groups, and reducing support for groups and their leaders. Jerrold M. Post, "Psychological Operations and Counterterrorism," *Joint Forces Quarterly*, No. 37, 2nd quarter 2005, p. 106. Post's four elements fall naturally within what Gray identifies as essential for counterterrorism policy.

150. Committee on Foreign Relations, U.S. Senate, *Embassies as Command Posts in the Anti-Terror Campaign*, S. Prt. 109-52, Report to Members, 109th Congress, 2nd Session, Washington, DC: U.S. Government Printing Office, December 15, 2006, p. 2.

151. Ginny Hill, "Military Focuses on Development in Africa," *Christian Science Monitor*, June 22, 2007, p. 7.

152. *Ibid*.

153. I thank Lieutenant Colonel Bouchat for bringing this excellent point to my attention.

154. The quotation is from Army Special Forces Captain Bill Torrey in Robert D. Kaplan, *Hog Pilots, Blue Water Grunts: The American Military in the Air, At Sea, and On the Ground*, New York: Random House, 2007, p. 308.

155. Perl, pp. 11-12.

156. As Robert D. Kaplan points out, Great powers are measured "by their ability and willingness to use their comprehensive military, economic, and political power. . . ." Kaplan, *Hog Pilots, Blue Water Grunts*, p. 301.

157. For a brief opinion, see Donovan C. Chau, "Democracy in Africa Depends on Countries' Vibrant Civil Societies," *Christian Science Monitor*, December 1, 2005, p. 8.

158. Christopher H. Varhola and Laura R. Varhola, "Avoiding the Cookie-Cutter Approach to Culture: Lessons Learned from Operations in East Africa," *Military Review*, Vol. 86, No. 6, November-December 2006, p. 76. The entire article is informed, persuasive, and highly recommended.

159. Gregory L. Joachim, "Draining the Swamp or Feeding the Crocodiles in Subsaharan Africa? " *Orbis*, Vol. 49, No. 1, Winter 2005, p. 161.

160. Post, p. 110.

161. L. H. Gann and Peter Duignan, *Africa South of the Sahara: The Challenge to Western Security*, Stanford, CA: Stanford University Press, 1981, p. 102.

162. Boré, p. 110.

163. Office of International Security Affairs.

164. A question posed to me at a seminar in Cairo, Egypt, May 20, 2007.

165. Darrick B. Lee, "DoD, International Agencies Work to Shape Strategic Effectiveness in Africa," U.S. European Command Press Release, July 9, 2007, available from *www.eucom.mil/english/News/main.asp?Yr=2007*, accessed July 11, 2007.